DATE DUE

Hydrangeas

Glyn Church

Photographs by Pat Greenfield

FIREFLY BOOKS

A FIREFLY BOOK

Published by Firefly Books Ltd., 2001

Second printing, 2002

National Library of Canada Cataloguing in Publication Data

Church, Glyn
    Hydrangeas

Includes bibliographical references and index.
ISBN 1-55209-571-1 (bound)
ISBN 1-55209-521-5 (pbk.)

1. Hydrangeas.   I. Greenfield, Pat.   II. Title.
SB413.H93C48 2001   635.9'3372
C00-931518-7

Publisher Cataloging-in-Publication Data (U.S.)

Church, Glyn.
    Hydrangeas / Glyn Church ; photographs by Pat Greenfield. —1st ed.
[96] p. : col. ill., col. photos., maps ;   cm.
Includes bibliographical references and index.
Summary: Complete guide to hydrangeas including: history, cultivation, propagation, garden design and detailed descriptions of more than 75 varieties.
ISBN 1-55209-571-1
ISBN 1-55209-521-5 (pbk.)
1. Hydrangeas. 2. Gardening. I. Greenfield, Pat. II. Title.
635.93/ 372 21   CIP   SB413.H93.C58 2001

Published in Canada in 2002 by
Firefly Books Ltd.
3680 Victoria Park Avenue
Toronto, Ontario M2H 3K1

Published in the United States in 2002 by
Firefly Books (U.S.) Inc.
P.O. Box 1338, Ellicott Station
Buffalo, New York 14205

Acknowledgments

I thoroughly enjoyed writing this book, it was a most enjoyable experience. I would like to thank everyone for their help and support, especially:
Graham Smith for instigating the book, Gail Church for her patience and help with flower colors. Tracey Borgfeldt, Joy Browne, Jane Rumble and Paul Bateman for editing and producing the book. Brian and Chris Evans, Roy Treherne, Maurice Foster, Corinne Mallet, Os Blumhardt, Donald McPherson, Ian McDowell, Ian and Sheryl Swan, Mark and Abbie Jury, Romayne Abraham, Sunshine Environmental, Vernon and Erica Harrison, Tony Barnes and John Sole for information, photos and plants, and thanks to Joni Mitchell for the music to write to.

A special thank you to Pat Greenfield for her brilliant photographs. It was a pleasure to work with you.

Page 1: Evening sky with hydrangea by the sea.
Page 2: Hydrangea in a herbaceous border.
Page 3: Hydrangea macrophylla 'Alpenglühen' (syn 'Alpenglow').

Cover design by Shelley Watson, Sublime Design
Book design by Errol McLeary
Typesetting by Jazz Graphics
Printed in Hong Kong through Colorcraft Ltd

Contents

Introduction

We all have this halcyon vision of summer – long hot sunny days, blue, blue skies and gardens full of dazzling flowers with a heady fragrance. In this ideal world our gardens are ablaze with color, full of lush perennials and big bold flowering shrubs – shrubs which are easy to grow, easy to prune, flower endlessly, suppress the weeds, and are never attacked by pests and diseases.

In the real garden world, the hydrangea is probably the only long-flowering summer shrub that comes close to this "perfect" description. Apart from roses and *Buddleia davidii*, to my mind no other frost hardy shrub even comes close to matching this ideal – and we all know roses need constant attention to thrive, requiring endless spraying and pruning, while buddleias are so successful they have become a weed in many places.

Hydrangeas will be improved by a light annual prune and an occasional feed. Otherwise they can be left alone to get on with the job of providing your garden with maximum color for minimal expense and effort. They will fill your beds and borders with fantastic flowers, subduing the weeds in the process, and yes, they are fragrant. Hydrangeas will bloom all summer long, during which time their heads can be cut for fresh flowers indoors. Just before the chills of winter arrive, you can cut and dry some of the flowerheads for long-lasting decoration.

Hydrangeas are a very diverse group of plants. You will be amazed at the range of varieties and colors now available, and by their versatility. Ideal for planting in pots, tubs, urns and windowboxes, hydrangeas make a magnificent display in outdoor living areas at the time these are most in use. Other types give the landscaper of larger gardens great

Hydrangea serrata 'Impératrice Eugénie'

opportunities to create mass plantings of incredible beauty, by water, in shade or sun, under trees, even climbing over walls and other structures.

These tough plants can be grown in a great range of garden situations. When most people think of hydrangeas, it is usually the big-leaved *Hydrangea macrophylla*, with their large round flowerheads, they have in mind. These macrophyllas are some of the most resilient garden shrubs, tolerating coastal winds and even wet or boggy soil where virtually all other shrubs would die. Some will tolerate shade as long as it is not too dry or dense. Most will grow in acid or alkaline (lime) soil, which is most unusual, as nearly all shrubs dislike lime.

Recent work by hybridists worldwide has meant a greatly increased range of both mophead and lacecap macrophylla hydrangeas is now available, and brings the genus once more into prominence. In the pages which follow, my aim has been to provide today's gardeners with up-to-date information about this classic shrub.

Hardiness Zone Map

This map has been prepared to agree with a system of plant hardiness zones that have been accepted as an international standard and range from 1 to 11. It shows the minimum winter temperatures that can be expected on average in different regions.

In this book, where a zone number has been given at the end of a hydrangea entry, the number corresponds with a zone shown here. That number indicates the coldest areas in which the particular plant is likely to survive through an average winter.

Note that these are not necessarily the areas in which it will grow best. Because the zone number refers to the minimum temperatures, a plant given zone 7, for example, will obviously grow perfectly well in zone 8, but not in zone 6. Plants grown in a zone considerably higher than the zone with the minimum winter temperature in which they will survive might well grow but they are likely to behave differently. Note also that some readers may find the numbers a little conservative; we felt it best to err on the side of caution.

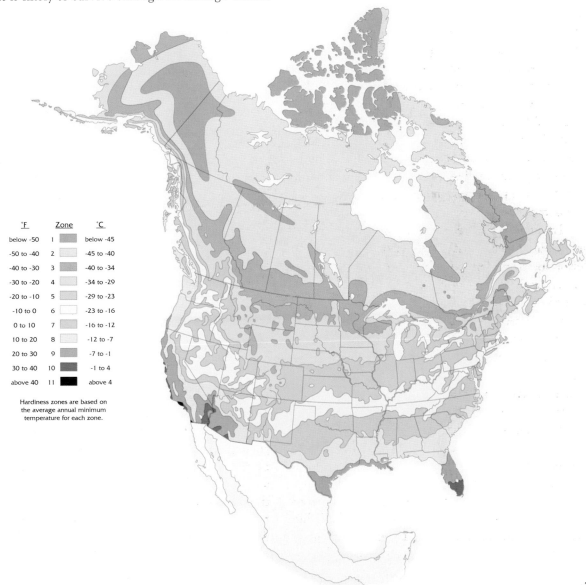

°F	Zone	°C
below -50	1	below -45
-50 to -40	2	-45 to -40
-40 to -30	3	-40 to -34
-30 to -20	4	-34 to -29
-20 to -10	5	-29 to -23
-10 to 0	6	-23 to -16
0 to 10	7	-16 to -12
10 to 20	8	-12 to -7
20 to 30	9	-7 to -1
30 to 40	10	-1 to 4
above 40	11	above 4

Hardiness zones are based on the average annual minimum temperature for each zone.

CHAPTER 1

Early History and Outline of the Genus

Hydrangeas have an interesting history. Not unusually, the story of their introduction to cultivation includes heroics, deprivation, mystery and intrigue. As with so many garden favorites, fans of hydrangeas should be grateful to some bold obsessive who risked life and limb to gather a new plant from the wild.

The first hydrangea to be discovered and introduced to gardens was the North American *Hydrangea arborescens*, collected by John Bartram in the 1730s, and described in *Flora Virginica* in 1739. John Bartram (1699-1777) was the son of a Quaker farmer who left England for the New World in 1680. The Bartram family are best summed up as a dogged and determined lot, traits not uncommon in new immigrants. However, John's father was not a fortunate man. He held strong personal opinions which led to his excommunication from his church and his community. A short while later his wife died, and he then left Pennsylvania for a new life in North Carolina, leaving his children, including young John, with their grandmother. His luck finally ran out when he was killed by Indians.

Like his father, the younger John Bartram was disowned by his church for his strong personal beliefs. Unlike his father, he chose to ignore the parish and took his usual place in church every week, to the congregation's embarrassment. An innovative man, he was a successful farmer who also raised a large family. Suddenly, after years of farming, he gave away respectability along with his plow.

Opposite: *Hydrangea macrophylla* 'Beauté Vendômoise'

Inspired by a chance purchase of a botanical tome, he remained obsessed with books and botany for the rest of his life. Botany totally consumed him and so he hired a man to take over his farming duties while he went plant-hunting – not an easy decision for a farmer with a large family to feed.

Bartram was lucky enough to make contact with a London merchant, Peter Collinson, who had been desperate to find a botanist in the colonies who would be willing to send him plants and seeds. Initially their relationship was akin to a love affair when both parties are unsure of the other's intentions and sincerity. Bartram was commissioned to send a box of plants and seeds to Collinson for five guineas. Delighted to be able to indulge his passion for botany and receive an income, he was doubtless hoping against hope that Collinson would want more boxes. Meanwhile, Collinson was equally keen for more boxes, but tempered his enthusiasm, having frightened off other senders with his zeal.

Eventually the "match" was made. Bartram sent hundreds of boxes during the next 30 years to the ever-enthusiastic Collinson. Traffic was not all one way. Bartram continually pestered Collinson to send him books on botany, a scarce commodity in the colonies.

In 1732, traveling for thousands of miles through the wilds of the Appalachian Mountains to as far south as Florida, alone and mostly on foot, this man was exploring the wilderness before Daniel Boone. Frontiersman Davy Crockett wasn't even born until after Bartram's death. Collinson meanwhile sold shares in Bartram's "boxes" to wealthy patrons, the landed gentry of England. Later, thanks to

Collinson's influence, Bartram was to win the honor of being "the King's Botanist" to George III. At this time the colonies were "The New World" and any new plant was regarded as a "treasure". (Even today people love "new" plants.) Both men became famous in their own country; Europeans credit Collinson with importing vast numbers of plants, while Americans regard Bartram as the "father of American botany".

Bartram made many long and arduous trips alone into dangerous Indian country. In later years his son William accompanied him on his travels and they discovered *Hydrangea quercifolia*, which is native to Georgia. Together they set up a five-acre botanic garden at Bartram's home on the Schuylkill River. Today this property is part of the Philadelphia Parks Department.

John Bartram died during the War of Independence, as General William Howe's troops were ravaging the countryside around Philadelphia after the battle of Brandywine. Among the wonderful plants he introduced to cultivation were *Magnolia acuminata*, *Magnolia grandiflora* (which sent his patron into ecstasy when it flowered for the first time), the extremely rare *Franklinia alatamaha* (a camellia relative) which is now extinct in the wild, and the Venus flytrap, *Dionaea muscipula*.

It is curious how plant-hunters always seem to be among the first people into any new country, closely followed by missionaries. Some of them were both plant-hunter and missionary, for example Père Armand David and Père Jean-Marie Delavay, French Catholic missionaries who collected literally thousands of plants in their "spare time" in China. Many of these early plant collectors were only interested in cataloging plants from a botanical viewpoint rather than sending them home for garden cultivation.

In 1587 the Japanese prohibited Catholic missionary priests and later on, in 1639, closed their borders to all foreigners, to secure their culture. Japan had witnessed the devastation Europeans had inflicted on North American and Pacific peoples and decided to ban all foreigners. Coinciding as it did with the era in which Europeans wanted to discover new lands, find new plants and make new converts to Christianity, this bar on foreigners led to conflict. As a concession, the Japanese allowed two nations to set up trading stations in their country, choosing the Dutch and Chinese because neither had sent missionaries to Japan. The Dutch East India Company settled a trading base on Deshima Island, an artificial island just offshore from Nagasaki.

Never ones to miss an opportunity, the trading companies were always on the lookout for new "economic" plants and who better to find them than botanists on the payroll. The Dutch East India Company employed a series of physicians whose skills included botany. The first of these was Engelbert Kaempfer (1651-1715), the first man to discover and describe the Asian hydrangeas, though he is rarely credited with this. He included them in the *Sambucus* or elderberry group of plants. Kaempfer found it extremely difficult to search for plants or botanize because the Japanese put severe travel restrictions on foreigners, and so it was only during his annual visit to Tokyo that he could go plant-hunting. A delegation from the company had to travel once a year to the Emperor's court to "prove their worthiness" to remain trading in Japan.

Nearly 100 years later Carl Peter Thunberg (1743-1828), a Swedish physician, held the same post with the Dutch East India Company and had to comply with the same travel restrictions. Frustrated at not being allowed off the island to search for new species, he devised a scheme to acquire mainland plants. Thunberg kept a goat and on the pretext of collecting fodder for this animal, his Japanese servants were allowed to go and "harvest" greenery and hay on the mainland. Among this "goat fodder" were two plants that he described as *Viburnum macrophyllum*, a tough coastal plant, and *Viburnum serratum*, a smaller woodland plant. It turned out

Viburnum sargentii with lacecap flowers similar to a hydrangea.

that these two plants were in fact hydrangeas, so when they were later transferred to the hydrangea genus, they kept the species names that Thunberg had used. Unknown to the doctor, hydrangeas had already been discovered in North America and were classified in their own genus. Viburnums share with hydrangeas the peculiarity of having large showy sterile flowers and small fertile flowers in the same flowerhead.

Philipp Franz von Siebold (1797-1866) was the next famous plant-hunter to get involved with hydrangeas. A German physician and eye specialist, he also worked for the Dutch East India Company, based in Deshima. His expertise allowed him onto the Japanese mainland to visit patients, on which occasions he casually "botanized" along the way. Based in Japan for six years from 1823 to 1829, he wrote a *Flora Iaponica* of Japanese plants and discovered several new species of hydrangea.

Siebold was enthralled by Japanese culture and this led to his downfall. He chose to live as a Japanese, endeavoring to learn as much as possible about the country's culture, geography and botany. Persuading a Japanese astronomer friend to part with a map of Japan and mainland Amur proved unwise. (The Japanese authorities considered maps secret documents, as part of their efforts to keep out foreigners.) On the short coastal voyage back to Deshima, Siebold's ship ran aground and the map was discovered. Some of those involved did not live to tell the tale. Siebold was imprisoned and eventually banished. He did not return to Japan for 30 years.

In 1859, when he was no longer *persona non grata*, Siebold had his wish granted when he was allowed to return as an adviser to the Japanese Government, which gave him independence from the East India

Company. To his joy, he was permitted to live on the mainland and botanize. However his newfound independence annoyed the Dutch and they demanded his recall, which he rejected. Three years after his initial appointment, the Company tricked him into traveling to Java for a diplomatic post that didn't exist. Once out of the country, they would not allow him to go back to Japan, so he returned home to Bavaria in disgust.

It was during his second sojourn in Japan that Siebold discovered and introduced *Hydrangea paniculata*. The doctor also unsuspectingly created a lot of botanical confusion by assuming that all the plants he found in Japanese nurseries and gardens were Japanese natives. In fact, many of these were from China, for there was already an exchange of plants between that country and Japan.

In one confusing issue of country of origin, a hydrangea was involved. This was collected on the Chinese mainland and introduced to England. There it was assumed to be a Chinese native plant and called *Hydrangea macrophylla* "Sir Joseph Banks" after the famous explorer and botanist who traveled the South Seas with Captain Cook and who, on his return, was responsible for the establishment of Kew Gardens. This cultivar is still in garden catalogs today.

Move on a little to 1879 when the famous Veitch Nursery in Exeter, England, sent Charles Maries to China and Japan to collect garden-worthy plants. He brought back two hydrangeas from Japan. One was a form of the coastal *Hydrangea macrophylla* with a lacecap flower; this was called *H.m.* "Mariesii", after the collector. The other was a round, dome-headed form of *Hydrangea serrata* and was named *H.s.* "Rosea". Neither of these plants caused much excitement in England but Monsieur A. Truffaut took them to France where they were exhibited at the Société Nationale d'Horticulture in Paris in 1901. From that point on French horticulturists bred hydrangeas with gusto. Subsequently Belgian, German and Swiss breeders joined the quest for the perfect hydrangea – perfection supposedly being good performance as a pot plant. Many were bred for forcing as early summer-flowering pot plants for sale throughout Europe and in fact this trade is still viable today.

In 1902 the French Lemoine brothers discovered that mophead hydrangeas have a few true flowers within and they set about breeding them. Subsequently other French nurserymen, Messrs Mouillère and Cayeux, joined the race to breed new exotic hydrangeas for indoor decoration. This explains why so many of the popular hydrangeas have such long French names, e.g. "Générale Vicomtesse de Vibraye" and "Souvenir du Président Paul Doumer". (Nowadays a cultivar is only allowed three names for the sake of simplicity and brevity, and so the latter is sold as "Président Doumer".)

It was only later discovered just how frost hardy hydrangeas are. There was a tendency early last century, especially in England, to regard any plant from exotic shores as frost tender. One only has to look at 1950s plant encyclopedias, which describe many a frost hardy plant as only fit for greenhouse culture, to see how the myth persisted. This partly accounts for hydrangeas being ignored by English-speaking plant breeders.

You may wonder why hydrangeas were not treasured by the Japanese, who have been such creative gardeners for centuries. Two reasons are put forward: the hydrangea is a fast-growing deciduous plant not suited to the tight clipping regime of a Japanese garden; and its habit of changing flower color from summer to fall and, in some species, changing color according to the soil, makes the plant fickle in Japanese eyes and therefore not suitable.

Opposite: *Hydrangea macrophylla* 'Générale Vicomtesse de Vibraye'

The hydrangea plant family

Where do hydrangeas come from? We've seen that frost hardy hydrangeas occur naturally in Japan, China and eastern North America, along the Appalachian Mountains. There are a surprisingly large number of plants that come from these three regions. Before the continents drifted apart, the Appalachian mountain chain was an island situated near what is now China and Japan, which may account for the common plant genera. Other plants based in all three regions are *Clethra*, *Illicium* and *Hamamelis*.

Some hydrangea species grow in outlying areas from these three core regions – in Vietnam, the Philippines, Mexico and South America. Most of these have never made it into cultivation in the West because they are too frost tender for our climate.

Hydrangeas have few relatives in the plant world and belong to their very own plant family – Hydrangeaceae. There are some choice but rather rare relatives of hydrangea that are discussed in Chapter 4.

Plant names

Most plants have just two names: a genus name such as "Hydrangea", which is like our surname, and a species name such as "macrophylla", which is like our given names, to distinguish us from others in the same household. The genus and species names are always written in italic type, with an initial capital for the genus only. Occasionally a plant has three names, such as *Hydrangea aspera* var *villosa* and *Hydrangea aspera* var *sargentiana*. This third name is called a subspecies because, according to botanists, both *H. aspera* var *villosa* and *H. aspera* var *sargentiana* are so similar botanically they do not warrant a species name of their own. From a gardener's point of view they look quite different and are easily distinguished. This anomaly arises because botanists are only interested in the flower construction and shape, whereas gardeners are interested in flowers but also in color, leaf shape and overall plant shape and form. In some older books you will find these two hydrangeas under their old

names of *H. villosa* and *H. sargentiana*. Notice how the genus is abbreviated to just *H.* and we can also shorten the species name to a letter and write *H.a.* var *villosa* instead of *Hydrangea aspera* var *villosa*.

A cultivar or plant form is found either in the wild or in cultivation and is considered an improvement on the ordinary version of the wild plant. Botanists would not consider the flower different enough to warrant a species or subspecies name, but from a gardener's point of view it is sufficiently different to be desirable. A cultivar has to be propagated by cutting or grafting. If seed is collected and planted, the resulting seedling would revert to the usual wild form. An example is *H. paniculata* 'Grandiflora'.

Hybrids are the result of cross-pollination between two plants. This pollination can be deliberate or can happen naturally. The seed that results from the cross-pollination will give rise to many different plants. If the best is selected and named it is called a clone and then has to be propagated by cuttings or grafts to keep the good qualities. These are usually called varieties, e.g. *H. macrophylla* 'Harlequin'. Most of the *Hydrangea macrophylla* varieties are hybrids bred by French, German or Swiss breeders.

Above: Flowers of *Rosa* 'Gold Medal' showing protective bracts around bud to the left. Above left: *Hydrangea macrophylla* 'Libelle'

Hydrangea flowers

Hydrangeas are quite different from most flowers, for they do not have showy petals. Take a rose, for example, and you will find showy colorful flowers made up of petals. Before the rose flower opens, it is protected in the bud stage by tough green bracts or "sepals" which make up the outer casing or bud. Hydrangeas don't have petals and so they have turned the sepals into "pretend petals".

The showy bits we think of as a hydrangea's flowers are actually bracts or sepals. These sepals take the place of petals, serving the same purpose as the petals in other flowers. They are the showy colorful parts that attract insects to the flower. The big mophead hydrangea flowers are actually made up of infertile or sterile flowers. Most flowers use showy colorful petals and/or scent to attract insects such as bees to pollinate the flower and produce seeds. Hydrangeas use both these ploys.

The key word when considering hydrangea flowers is **sepals**. The flowers with big sepals are sterile so they cannot produce seeds. In the case of hydrangeas the "true" flowers with all the sexual parts are very small. These true flowers are fertile and are capable of producing seeds.

Hydrangea flowerheads come in various shapes and forms. Most of us visualize *Hydrangea macrophylla* when we think of hydrangeas. These are divided into two shapes – mopheads and lacecaps.

Mopheads are made up of lots of sterile flowers and just a tiny few fertile flowers hidden within. The reason the heads last so long is because the flowers are sterile and do not have to produce fruits and seeds. (Most other flowers drop their petals once they've been pollinated and begin the task of producing seeds.)

Lacecaps, the second type, have a flat plate-like flower which has a row or two of big sepal flowers around the rim and a mass of tiny true flowers in the middle of the plate. The name "lacecap" comes from

Above: Lacecap with ring of sterile flowers surrounding the true seed-producing flowers.

Below: A mophead hydrangea made up of sterile flowers.

Outer flowers on a lacecap turn over and change color in fall. This is *H.m.* 'Nightingale', which was rich blue in summer. The yellow daisy is *Ligularia* 'Desdemona'.

the lace caps that servant girls used to wear in the stately homes of Europe.

Hydrangeas have two types of flower. Within each flowerhead there is usually a mix of fertile (true) and infertile (sterile) flowers. Some hydrangea flowers are a mixture of the two and some have only fertile (true) or only infertile (sterile) flowers. Most plants have true flowers to carry out the essential work of producing seeds and use the ornamental petals to attract insects to do the pollinating.

Hydrangeas have one set of flowers to attract the insects and another completely different set to produce the seeds. The true flowers, which are fertile and produce the seeds, are shaped like a vessel and this gives the name "hydrangea", as the seed capsule is shaped like a Greek water vessel. Two Greek words make up hydrangea: *hydra* = water and *angeion* = a vessel.

If you open up the petals on a mophead hydrangea you will find a few true or fertile flowers within. Hydrangeas are outstanding because they

flower for such a long period. Even a rosebush that flowers all summer is not presenting the same flowers all the time, for they open in succession. With hydrangeas, the flowers open and go on and on and on all summer, and part of the reason for this is that the sterile or ray flowers cannot be pollinated and so the "show" continues.

The true flowers in the center of a lacecap will be pollinated and gradually change color and become seed pods. When this happens, the large sterile flowers rotate and change color, which adds another dimension to the flowers.

The flowers do not last as long on the lacecaps, because after pollination the plant begins to put energy into making seeds. At this point the larger sterile florets turn 180 degrees and change color, say from white to pink. Their flowering season can be measured in weeks instead of months.

Most of the wild (i.e. species) hydrangeas have lacecap-type flowers, though a few have panicles of flowers. These are long pointed flowerheads where the flowers open in succession, with the oldest at the base. *Hydrangea quercifolia* and *Hydrangea paniculata* both have panicles. The name "paniculata" comes from the latin name for "panicle".

CHAPTER 2

Wild Hydrangea Species and Cultivated Forms

Hydrangea arborescens

Hydrangea arborescens (commonly called the smooth hydrangea or American hydrangea) is one of the two North American species. It has the distinction of being the first hydrangea to be introduced into cultivation. The name "arborescens" means "tree-like", and in the wild it can grow to 10 ft (3 m), but it is usually only just over 3 ft (1 m) high in a garden. Many of the Chinese species are distinctly more tree-like than *H. arborescens*, but they were discovered much later.

In the wild this wide-ranging species is found from New York State all through the Appalachian Mountains down to Florida, growing in shady, moist sites. It can be a little difficult to please in warm, moist climates unless attention is paid to good drainage to prevent root rot. It seems to tolerate moist sites in a cooler climate. All forms of *H. arborescens* will endure severe cold, tolerating harsh winters up to Zone 3. They are also very drought-resistant. Some forms are likely to sucker, sending up new plants from underground. This is rarely a problem and easily controlled, and may be put to good use to propagate new plants.

The wild form has a small lacecap flower in subdued white. There are two subspecies. All three are equally happy in sun or shade and are rarely attacked by pests and diseases.

Hydrangea arborescens subsp radiata (silverleaf hydrangea) has more garden merit than *H. arborescens*, forming a large upright tidy shrub. The sweetly scented large white lacecaps, held well

Hydrangea arborescens radiata

above the bush, are displayed attractively. The splendid heart-shaped leaves are slightly hairy above and covered in velvety silver hairs on the reverse. This is a charming woodland plant for larger gardens. It grows to 10 ft (3 m).

Hydrangea arborescens discolor is another wild form with a white lacecap flower and slightly hairy leaves. It grows to 10 ft (3 m).

The two garden varieties of *Hydrangea arborescens* below are well worth growing as excellent replacements for mophead hydrangeas in colder climates.

H. arborescens 'Grandiflora' has slightly uneven, almost pointed mopheads of pure white sterile flowers. This plant looks truly beautiful when established, though it does have an untidy weeping habit in the early years. It blooms from mid to late summer, grows to 5 ft (1.5 m) and makes an excellent cut flower.

H. arborescens 'Annabelle' (also 'Hills of Snow') is a marvelous form recently popularized in North America. Very large heads of white sterile flowers make this an outstanding shrub for any garden. The flowerheads can be so heavy it is impossible for the shrub to keep them upright. Some people recommend severe pruning every winter to encourage strong new growth that can support the huge blooms. Eventually, as the plant gets bigger, this problem is solved by the bush holding a better shape as it gets stronger. 'Annabelle' needs a sheltered site away from wind because of the large blooms. It grows to 5 ft (1.5 m). This hydrangea makes a very good cut flower and is much more showy than the species plant but it lacks the grace of the wild plant.

Hydrangea aspera

Hydrangea aspera is a little known species from China. So why mention it at all? Well, the botanists who choose the Latin names of a plant have decided this species now includes lots of popular garden hydrangeas previously known under names like *H. sargentiana* and *H. villosa*. These are now all classified as subspecies of *H. aspera*. In its true form *H. aspera* is a variable plant with hairy leaves and lacecap flowers, often with muddy-colored sterile flowers. It is robust and easy to grow, eventually reaching 10 ft (3 m) or more. Unfussy about soils and happy in full sun or semi-shade, it is frost hardy to Zone 7 and suffers from virtually no pest or disease problems. Gardeners should seek out the named forms as they are truly beautiful.

H. aspera var sargentiana – those of you who have been fans of hydrangeas for a few years may be puzzled by the name changes. This used to be a species in its own right but is now regarded by botanists as a subspecies of *H. aspera*. *H. aspera* var *sargentiana* was named after Charles Sargent of Arnold Arboretum fame. He was a plant-collector in Japan and later classified the plants of Ernest Wilson, who was probably the most successful plant-hunter of all time. Wilson collected this plant in China and it is considered one of the choicest hydrangeas, sought after by many gardening enthusiasts. Having said that, it is rather rare and can be difficult to cultivate. It is also tricky to propagate, which adds to the scarcity value. As well as being difficult to grow from cuttings, it produces very few stems, unlike most hydrangeas. In winter the few thick bare stems it does produce look rather like deer antlers, with thick bristly hairs all along the branches.

So why is this variety so desired by gardeners? The large lacecap flowers have pink-hued white sterile flowers surrounding smoky mauve to lilac true flowers. The main appeal, however, lies in the huge bristly leaves that allow it to compare favorably with the giant rhododendrons as a foliage plant. *H.a.*var

Hydrangea aspera

Hydrangea arborescens 'Annabelle'

sargentiana forms a very big suckering shrub that is suitable for large gardens and parks. It grows to 7-10 ft (2-3 m).

Now to the tricky part – growing this successfully. It needs to be in shade to protect the big leaves from damaging winds and hot sun. Ideally a mulch of well-rotted leaves or compost on the soil surface will keep the roots moist, though it does like good drainage. Plant it at the back of a border under the shade of a tall and lacy maple such as *Acer negundo* and maybe some *Hydrangea macrophylla* in front with their big smooth leaves as a contrast, or alternatively some *Sarcococca* with smooth glossy green leaves. If you succeed in growing this hydrangea you will be the envy of your neighbors.

H. aspera var villosa A favorite of mine, this bears pink and mauve lacecap flowers throughout late summer. It grows up to 10 ft (3 m) in full sun or just a morsel of shade. Planted at the back of a border, with a dark backdrop of evergreen shrubs, when in full flower this will gladden the heart of any true gardener. The hairy narrow leaves have a tinge of color and are held till late in the fall but have no noticeable color change.

It is pleasing to report this species is very easy to grow, and the only factor which may prevent it being included in every garden is its ultimate size. Some people may think 10 ft (3 m) is too tall, but if you have room for large shrubs then do make space for one of these. Think of it as a 7 ft (2 m) shrub, as it takes a long time to reach its full height, and then you can enjoy it for many years and if it eventually becomes too big for your garden, you will find it impossible to live without. Of fairly dense structure and very full-looking, this hydrangea is reasonably

Above: *Hydrangea aspera* var *villosa*

Above right: *Hydrangea heteromalla*

drought resistant and succeeds in hot dry conditions. It tolerates alkaline soil, and is more likely to die of poor drainage than frost. Cold hardy, growing to Zone 7, *H.a.* var *villosa* has leaves and stems which are densely villous and this hairy foliage protects it against wind and cold. It was collected in western China by E.H. Wilson.

Hydrangea heteromalla

Hydrangea heteromalla (Himalayan hydrangea) can be very tall and elegant. It is variable, depending on the seed source. Usually the sterile flowers of the lacecap are white or pink surrounding off-white to green true flowers. Handsome forms with huge hairy leaves and pink and mauve flowers are sometimes available. Some even have flowers in tiers of multiple lacecaps up to an enormous 2 ft (60 cm) wide. These multiple flowerheads can have up to eight lacecaps in one huge flower. This hydrangea is really only suitable for large gardens or parks as it eventually reaches 16 ft (5 m). *H. heteromalla* is reasonably hardy, growing to Zone 6, though some of the larger-leaved forms with huge flowers are very frost tender and need Zones 9 to 10. This hydrangea is happy in sun or part shade and is rarely attacked by pests or fungi.

Hydrangea macrophylla

Hydrangea macrophylla is the type most people picture when hydrangeas are mentioned. This species is undoubtedly the most popular and well known of all the hydrangeas. The name "macrophylla" means "big leaf", (macro = big, and phylla = leaf), referring to their very large, bold leaves. They are often called mophead or big leaf hydrangeas and may be incorrectly listed as *Hydrangea hortensia* (hortensias and garden hortensias). The lacecap types are also called thus, and can sometimes be cited as *H.m* var *normalis*.

Hydrangea macrophylla comes originally from Japan and has caused botanists much confusion. Some believe it is a naturally occurring species while others maintain it is of hybrid origin. The plants in cultivation under the name of *H. macrophylla* 'Seafoam' and the one that J.P. Commerson introduced as *H. opuloides* (now *H. macrophylla*) seem to be close enough to the real species, coming true when sown from seed.

These are naturally coastal plants in their native Japan and even grow right by the sea. The tough glossy leaves make them an excellent coastal dweller

and this is part of the reason they became popular as shrubs for seaside gardens. Of the many hybrids, some have inherited this ability to cope with coastal conditions. They are resilient plants, tolerating shade, sun, wet soil and virtually anything the elements and gardeners can throw at them, including frost, though this may cause growth to weaken or the plant to lose flowers for the coming summer. They are quite hardy growing from Zones 5 and 6 through to Zone 10.

Naturally they have a lacecap flower, with white to the palest flax-blue sterile florets and true flowers of dark sea-blue.

The mophead types were just a naturally occurring "sport". (A sport is created when a part of a plant naturally mutates and becomes a different looking plant, which is then propagated by cuttings. Most of the conifers with yellow or blue foliage, also the dwarf conifers, began as branch sports on bigger trees which were removed and propagated.) In the case of hydrangeas, breeders have taken these mophead sports and bred from them to produce more colorful mopheads. Hydrangeas 'Ayesha', 'Otaksa' and 'Sir Joseph Banks' are probably sports of the (species) *Hydrangea macrophylla*. Chapter 3 deals with cultivars of *H. macrophylla*.

Hydrangea paniculata

Hydrangea paniculata (panicle hydrangea or tree-/tree-form hydrangea) deserves a place in every garden. In late summer the bush is covered in huge frothy white flowers, the panicles being made up of large, creamy white sterile and small fertile flowers. The proportion of sterile and fertile flowers varies with each form or cultivar.

Hardier than most species, *H. paniculata* will tolerate extreme cold – growing to Zone 3. It is not fussy about the soil type as long as the drainage is reasonable. Like most shrubs, it prefers a well-drained, moist soil, but it will grow in clay or rocky ground.

The height of the bush varies and can reach the size of a small tree, growing up to 20 ft (6 m), though most cultivated bushes are more like 7 ft (2 m). It is best grown in full sun and a sheltered site. The stems are brittle and easily broken by strong winds. This is an easy-care plant, untouched by diseases or pests. Some forms make wonderful cut flowers. The larger heavier-blooming types have such weighty flowers that an arching shrub is created when the branches are fully laden.

A native of Japan and southeast China, *H. paniculata* was first introduced to western cultivation by Philipp von Siebold.

H. paniculata 'Floribunda' bears a cone of frothy white flowers consisting of a mix of true and sterile flowers. All the sterile flowers tend to face outwards from the central cone and go pink as the summer progresses. This hydrangea forms a tall plant, sometimes up to 16 ft (5 m) and so needs fairly drastic pruning each winter to be feasible for a small garden. It looks spectacular in a large garden as an isolated specimen, or at the back of a border.

H. paniculata 'Grandiflora' was introduced from Japan by Siebold. It is probably the best known version of *H. paniculata* and goes by the common name of 'Pee Gee'. It bears huge triangular flowerheads of sterile flowers that are so heavy the branches

Hydrangea paniculata 'Grandiflora'

bend over with their weight. Sometimes the branches are so heavy with the weight of the flowers that they break in a strong wind, so, probably more than any other, this form needs good shelter. Flower cones can be up to 18 in (45 cm) long and 12 in (30 cm) wide at the base. The blooms are a lovely creamy-white, opening to pure white before turning pinky shades as fall approaches. Flowers can be successfully cut for dried arrangements at that time.

It is possible to cut *H.p.* 'Grandiflora', to ground level every year in a herbaceous border, as it flowers on new wood. An excellent subject for a mixed border, or as an informal group, this hydrangea can be left to grow into a very large upright shrub (height 10 ft or 3 m), or you can drastically prune it every winter to keep the bush within bounds and to increase the size of the flowers.

H. paniculata 'Kyushu' A lovely dainty form of the species collected on Kyushu Island in Japan by Collingwood Ingram, this hydrangea makes a much smaller bush than the species (height 5 ft or 1.5 m) and has smaller heads of flowers, which are very showy. Its size makes it ideal for smaller gardens and it produces a wonderful contrast when planted with purple or bronze forms of *Acer palmatum*.

H. paniculata 'Pink Diamond' This plant's main claim to fame is the tendency of the mass of sterile flowers to change to pink during the summer. Most *H. paniculata* types tend to go pink as summer wanes, but 'Pink Diamond' starts showing pink tinges almost as soon as the flowers emerge. The sterile flowers eventually become more rosy, almost red in color. It grows to 7 ft (2 m). Plant in a sunny site to enhance the color change.

H. paniculata 'Praecox' is a personal favorite, being such a graceful garden shrub (height 8 ft or 2.5 m). "Praecox" means "early" and the cones of frothy flowers emerge in early summer. Because the heads are a combination of true and sterile flowers, they are not too heavy and so the bush keeps its upright habit. Planted at the back of a border with dwarf bronze Japanese maples in front, this hydrangea creates a garden picture no one can resist. This slightly frost tender form was introduced from Japan by Charles Sargent.

H. paniculata 'Tardiva' (syn 'Compact Pee Gee') One of the many prized forms of *H. paniculata* which have become available in recent times, this tends to flower late in the season. Each panicle has a tidy, shapely appearance, with the bulk of the sterile flowers near its base. It grows best in Zones 6 to 7.

H. paniculata 'Unique' bears a huge panicle of flowers, even larger than *H.p.* 'Grandiflora', though the flower tends to be more rounded at the end. The mass of sterile flowers are so packed together that

Hydrangea paniculata 'Kyushu'

the impression is of being full to overflowing. The heads take on a pink or even rusty red appearance late in the season. It grows to 10-13 ft (3-4 m).

Hydrangea quercifolia

Hydrangea quercifolia is found in the southern states of eastern U.S.A. It is commonly called the oak leaf hydrangea and is native to Georgia, Florida and Mississippi. It is equally suited to inland or coastal regions, though best not planted too close to the sea as it is not as wind tolerant as the macrophylla types. The name "quercifolia" comes from the oak – quercus – because it has a leaf similar to the American red oaks. It is one of the most handsome hydrangeas, with big bold lobed leaves that turn rich crimson and purple in late fall. The exciting scarlet and crimson oak-shaped leaves are best achieved in full sun, and effectively set off the scrumptious flowers, which appear from mid-summer. These large triangular cones of creamy white blossoms take on pinkish tinges as fall approaches.

Like many other hydrangeas, *H. quercifolia* is a wonderful cut flower and useful for drying. It grows around 5 ft (1.5 m) high and up to 7 ft (2 m) wide, preferring a rich, moist but well-drained soil. It tolerates both acidic and alkaline soils and will survive more poorly drained conditions but does not like to be in a dry climate. It can sucker a little but this is rarely a problem as it doesn't become rampant and new plants are easily propagated. *H. quercifolia* is best grown in a sunny site as too much shade will suppress the bush and reduce the number of flowers, but a morsel of shade will be fine in a hot climate. One drawback is that this hydrangea can be attacked by root rot, which causes the plant to decline or even die. Otherwise it seems to be free of pests and diseases.

H. quercifolia grows happily in Zones 9 and 10 and needs some protection in cooler areas; planting against a sunny wall will be sufficient. It is hardy to Zone 6, provided it has warm summers to ripen the wood in preparation for the cold winter, but really requires a hot summer to flower well.

Although hardy through most of Britain, for example, it rarely thrives because the summers are not warm enough. In cooler regions, site it in a hot spot, maybe near the house, to help it perform well. Equally at home in a mixed border or a woodland setting, the oak-leafed hydrangea can also be grown in large tubs. The flowers have a delicate but attractive fragrance.

Hydrangea quercifolia 'Snow Flake'

Hydrangea quercifolia 'Snow Queen'

Hydrangea quercifolia 'Snow Flake' (syn 'Snow White') is a superb double-flowered form. In fact, the spirals of sterile flowers make this almost a quadruple flower. Not only is the flower a great improvement, but the plant has a better constitution than the species. This hydrangea provides interest almost all year round: the fabulous white double flowers change to rosy pink and even look good when dried in the winter and its fall color is superb, being a combination of wine-red to maroon, with brighter reds and orange for good measure. It is a plant that looks good combined with other shrubs or perennials, but is also attractive enough to be a garden focal point. It makes a real impact if surrounded by a gray groundcover to show off the fall color, or purple-leaved ajuga to highlight the flowers. It forms a 3 ft (1 m) slightly arching shrub, the tumbling habit enhanced by the weight of the flowers. As with the species, it needs warm summers to thrive.

Hydrangea quercifolia 'Snow Queen' is notable as a very showy single-flower form. The individual creamy white flowers are much larger than that of the species and it has foliage of exceptional fall color. It does, however, have an iffy constitution and can be difficult to grow.

Other named forms of *Hydrangea quercifolia* include 'Harmony', 'Sikes Dwarf' and 'Pee Wee', a splendid new dwarf form.

Hydrangea serrata

The name indicates this species has leaves with a jagged edge like a serrated knife. This lovely hydrangea hails from Japan and Korea where it is found in woods and forests. It is also known as the Tree-of-Heaven hydrangea or mountain hydrangea. *Hydrangea serrata* types are similar to *H. macrophylla* and can be used in the same way. The only thing is, they are not quite so robust and tolerant of windy or hot situations. In general they are smaller growing than the macrophyllas and therefore more suitable for smaller suburban gardens. Their delightful habit of three or four color changes per season means your summer garden will never be boring. Some of these, such as 'Impératrice Eugénie' and 'Preziosa' go through these same color changes regardless of the acidity of the soil and so they are more predictable than the macrophyllas. If you have a shady spot, the plants providing these color changes will captivate you all

Hydrangea serrata acuminata

through summer. They do tend to burn or scorch if in too hot or dry a position.

Generally *H. serrata* only grows to around 3 ft (1 m) high, so it fits easily into any garden. The species has flattened lacecap flowers with white, pink or blue ray florets or sterile flowers surrounding blue or white true flowers in the center of the head. It tolerates most soils, as long as they are not too alkaline, nor too wet. Hardy to Zone 6, this species is more fussy regarding conditions than *H. macrophylla*, not being happy in coastal gardens, or in full sun, where the flowers will crisp and dehydrate. However, this hydrangea is reasonably tolerant of frosts. Pests and diseases are few and far between, powdery mildew being the only one of any consequence.

There are some remarkable forms and hybrids of *H. serrata* that are worth growing (see Chapter 3).

Climbing hydrangeas

Hydrangea anomala subsp petiolaris
A deciduous climber that is hardy to Zone 4, *Hydrangea petiolaris* can be used in a multitude of ways. It looks fantastic climbing up a tree as it clothes the entire trunk, surrounding it with white lacecap flowers in early summer.

This species is not too fussy about soil, which is just as well as climbers often get planted in poor soil next to a wall or tree trunk. As it is happy in full sun or shade, *H. petiolaris* can be used to cover unsightly walls, fences and sheds. The roots do cling like ivy, so be aware they may later cause you problems if you want to paint the surface. I've seen this climbing hydrangea used to great effect on the outsides of city houses and hotels, or on old limestone farm walls, even as a groundcover to disguise an unsightly tree stump.

Last but not least, these climbers can be used to ascend trees, but have a care. Like most climbers,

they will grow as high as they can. If given a 7-ft (2 m) fence, they will climb 7 ft and then flower. If given a 70-ft (20 m) tree to climb, then they will grow 70 ft and take much longer to bloom and most of the flowers will be near the top! This same habit is true of most climbers, so when people say "Don't grow such and such. It grows 70 ft high", bear in mind this is only because the plant has been given a 70-ft tree to climb.

Hydrangea seemannii
A rare climber from Mexico, also known as the evergreen hydrangea, was introduced to gardens in the 1960s. *Hydrangea seemannii* needs a warm Zone 9 climate, free of major frosts. (It's generally easier to keep climbers free from frost as they grow vertically and often get the benefit of the warmth from a wall. Buildings give off heat at night and thus also help reduce the effects of frost.)

Set in dark green, glossy evergreen foliage, the flowerbuds drop their creamy white bracts to reveal a mass of white fertile flowers with a circle of sterile ones. It's not tidy enough to be described as a lacecap, rather it could be called an irregular collection of sterile and fertile flowers.

A collector's piece, *H. seemannii* tends to bloom best in warm climates.

Hydrangea serratifolia
A vigorous evergreen climber from Chile and Argentina, this is another that prefers a warm Zone 9 climate and needs heat to bloom well and keep off frosts. It displays bundles of fluffy white fertile flowers and is quite showy in a warm climate.

Schizophragma hydrangeoides
A relative of hydrangeas, these climbers look very similar to most gardeners and their common name is Japanese hydrangea vine or Japanese hydrangea. The lacecap flowers are a little larger than those of *Hydrangea petiolaris*, but there are less of them. *Schizophragma* cling with the same ivy-like roots as

Schizophragma hydrangeoides 'Roseum'

H. petiolaris. The flowers can be the size of small plates and consist of showy creamy heads. The heart-shaped leaves have a reddish tinge to the outside serrated edges.

Content in sun or shade, *S. hydrangeoides* flowers best in sun and is tolerant of hot summers, this frost hardy deciduous climber is happy up to Zone 5. It hails from Japan.

Schizophragma hydrangeoides 'Roseum' is a pretty form with rosy-colored bracts. The outer sepals also have a rosy tinge, adding an extra dimension.

Schizophragma integrifolium
This Chinese species is a little less frost hardy than the above, only tolerating Zones 7 to 10. The grayish furry leaves are heart-shaped and the creamy white lacecaps are huge (up to 12 in or 30 cm wide). The plant has fewer flowers to compensate for the huge size of each bloom. It is happy in long hot summers.

CHAPTER 3

Cultivars *of* Hydrangea macrophylla *and* H. serrata

Hydrangea macrophylla forms

*H*ydrangea macrophylla are quite frost hardy and, unless otherwise stated in the entries listed below, they generally grow from Zones 5 and 6 to Zone 10.

'Adria' Small blue heads on a very compact bush make this an ideal plant for small gardens. It flowers well and is suitable for all regions. Can be used for forcing for early flowers and as a container plant. The name comes from the Adriatic Sea, and so, as you would expect, it is a good sea-blue. It is not suitable for alkaline soils and grows to 3 ft (1 m).

'Alpenglühen' (syn 'Alpenglow', 'Glowing Embers', purple hydrangea, double red hydrangea, French hydrangea) A choice rosy-red mophead, even in slightly acidic soil. The nicely shaped, rounded head sits up well on the plant. A robust easy variety to grow, so if you're wanting a red mophead for any soil except very acidic, this is the one for you. It grows to a medium height and has a good constitution.

'Altona' A plant for all gardens, this variety produces a good pink in lime and an excellent French blue in acidic soils. In soils that are neither strongly acidic nor alkaline, i.e. "neutral", 'Altona' has a charming combination of pinky mauve with white centers, with the more open older flowers tending to blue.

Opposite: Hydrangea macrophylla 'Altona'

Very floriferous, covered in large flowerheads which sometimes completely enshroud the bush, hiding all its leaves, 'Altona' is happy in sun or shade, and is one of the best varieties for windy or coastal gardens. It grows to 7 ft (2 m), with leaves that are very dark green and have serrated edges.

'Alotona' is one of the best hydrangeas for fall flower color. Turning a burnished red, this variety provides excellent dried material for winter decoration.

It is popular for growing in containers because of the wonderful color combinations and is happy in sun and by the sea. However, it does appear to be frost tender inland and so is not the best for cold climates.

'Amethyst' Late flowering violet-blue or soft pink small flowers with serrated sepals. Some of the flowers are double, which adds a sparkle. Of stout growth and with very deep green leaves, the bush needs to be in a prime site near the house to be admired and have the advantage of frost protection, as it is frost tender. It grows to 3 ft (1 m).

'Ami Pasquier' A small to medium-sized bush with small dense round heads of rich crimson to Tyrian purple, 'Ami Pasquier' produces new flowers all summer, which is a bonus.

One of the best crimson hydrangeas for alkaline soils, and pretty in acidic soil, its leaves turn red in fall, which is another bonus, as most macrophyllas have no fall color. It grows to 5 ft (1.5 m).

'Ayesha' (syn 'Silver Slipper') A remarkable and very different hydrangea, one of the few varieties which can be recognized at a glance, as the florets of three or four sepals are thick and fleshy and held in a cup shape. (I always imagine them as cake decorations.) In a neutral or limey soil the color is a beautiful white to soft shell-pink, gradually enriching to pinky mauve as the summer progresses.

Above: *Hydrangea macrophylla* 'Ami Pasquier'
Below: *Hydrangea macrophylla* 'Ayesha'

In acidic soils the flowers are very gentle mauve-lilac to blue.

'Ayesha' has very shiny bold leaves and is therefore an excellent shrub for coastal and windy sites, being more tolerant of salt and wind than most. Not a good plant for inland gardens with heavy frosts as it is frost tender. Occasionally a branch reverts to a typical macrophylla flower in soft shell-pink. It grows to 7 ft (2 m).

'Beauté Vendômoise' Here's a choice and underrated variety. It was bred back in 1909 by Emile Mouillère. The flowers form an uncommonly large lacecap with enormous sterile florets that can be up to 5 in (12 cm) wide! Despite the huge size of the blooms, the plant has a lot of charm. The sterile florets are the palest butterfly-blue in acidic soil and the softest pink in alkaline ground. These sometimes emerge through the true flowers, which to some eyes spoils the flat lacecap effect. The scented flowers are a bonus. The large strong bush (height 10 ft or 3 m) would look out of place in a small suburban garden but offers much potential for larger, informal and park-like landscapes.

'Blaumeise' (syns 'Blue Tit', 'Blue Billow', 'Blue Sky', 'Teller Blue') This is a Swiss "Teller" hybrid, which translated from the German "blaumeise" means "blue tit", a small European bird. "Teller" is a German word that means "plate", which is another way of describing flat lacecap flowers. Most of the Teller hybrids are named after European birds and sometimes appear under their English translation names.

Teller hybrids are considered by many people to be frost tender and not tolerant of cold winters but a lot depends on whether they are being grown in a "continental climate" or elsewhere. (See p. 64 for more advice on this.)

'Blaumeise' has large sterile smooth-edged florets surrounding the fertile flowers in true lacecap fashion. Brilliant cobalt-blue flowers encircle the pale turquoise or Persian blue true flowers. The heads are quite small and dainty, which makes this an ideal variety for small gardens as it bears close scrutiny. It grows to 7 ft (2 m).

'Blue Prince' ('Blauerprinz') This is one of my favorites. In an acidic soil it's a simply stupendous cobalt blue with very small round heads. The bush is small, say 3 ft (1 m), and so the flowers are in proportion to the plant. True, the flower color is a wishy-washy pink in alkaline soil, and this variety doesn't have the toughest constitution, but if you have acidic soil and you want a fantastic blue, then this is it. It makes an excellent cut flower.

'Blue Wave' This plant has glossy leaves that are rounded in shape, with rounded serrations; such foliage indicates it's ideal for coastal or windy sites. Very large, smoky pink to blue sterile florets offset the rich bluebird-blue sepals and dark blue true flowers. (The true flowers of the similar *Hydrangea* 'Mariesii' are paler.) The overall effect is of a very large flat lacecap. The plant needs a very acidic soil to become a real blue in the outer sepals and the flowers tend to go a muddy color as the season progresses.

This is a tall hardy plant (height 5-7 ft or 1.5-2 m) that is happy in sun or shade but has been superseded by the likes of 'Nightingale' for gardeners with a mild climate.

'Bodensee' A pink mophead well suited to growing in pots and tubs as it has a second flush of flowers late in the summer. It is a dense, compact plant that grows to 4 ft (1.2 m). Its dwarf habit, long flowering season and healthy nature make it an ideal garden shrub.

'Bouquet Rose' This is one of the oldest hybrid hydrangeas available. Although it has been super-

Hydrangea macrophylla 'Blue Wave'

seded in terms of strong colors, it still has a certain charm. In alkaline soils the mopheads are soft pink; they become a very pale pinky violet in acidic soil. In fall the flowers change into hues of green and violet, which makes it an excellent dried flower. Also, as it tends to change color long before most other varieties, it can be picked early in the season

Hydrangea macrophylla 'Bodensee'

for dried flowers. The rather weak stems tend to bow with the weight of the flowers but this somehow adds to the allure of the plant. It is a very frost hardy bush that grows to 7 ft (2 m). It is not everyone's first choice, but a valuable garden plant nonetheless.

'Domotoi' (syn French hydrangea) This delightful hydrangea is unique because the flowers are double. The overlapping sepals have a porcelain appearance, highlighted by the frilly edges. Ideal for small gardens as it grows to not much more than 3 ft (1 m) high. In acidic soil the flowers are a marvelous pale butterfly-blue. It is not recommended for alkaline soils and makes lovely cut flowers.

'Enziandom' (syn 'Gentian Dome') If I could only have one dark blue mophead hydrangea, then this would be the one. It produces the most scintillating gentian-blue in acidic soil. (If you don't have acidic soil then don't bother with it.) The bold sturdy plant stays quite compact – say 5 ft (1.5 m) – and forms strong stems topped with big wide heads of blue. There's a nice clean appearance to the flowerheads, which are dense domes made up of large smooth-

Hydrangea macrophylla 'Domotoi'

edged sepals, 10 in across and 5 in high (25 cm x 12 cm). It makes a great cut flower.

'Europa' Here's an unusual variety that tends to grow tall and rather straggly but produces a very agreeable pink mophead which becomes a passable mauve-blue in acidic soils. It does tend to be a muddy color in neutral soils and there are better varieties available. However, because of its vigor, it makes an excellent hedge or backdrop for a border, and the fall flower color looks great when dried.

'Fasan' (syn 'Pheasant', 'Twilight') A Teller lacecap that is best in alkaline soil, where it becomes bright red. "Fasan" is German for "pheasant", a bird with a bright red wattle on its head. The large sterile flowers, which are distinctly pointed, tend to be in a double row, almost masking the true flowers at times. This hydrangea is sensitive to late frost which can reduce the number of flowers. It forms a bold upright plant that grows up to 5 ft (1.5 m). In neutral soil the color is rather unattractive and muddy. Acidic soils produce pansy-violet-colored flowers.

'Freudenstein' Bearing large heads of excellent pink to Persian rose in alkaline soil, 'Freudenstein' becomes blue with a hint of purple in an acidic mix. It has very large florets with gaps between the sepals. The low dense bush (height 3 ft or 1 m) is ideal for tubs except that it's prone to mildew when stressed.

'Frillibet' Selected in the 1950s by Michael Haworth-Booth, an English hydrangea fanatic, the name is a play on the nickname "Lillibet" for Elizabeth. It forms a dense bush just over a 4 ft (1 m) high with large flattened heads. The flowers are a very, very soft blue, gradually taking on a more blue coloration as the summer progresses. In the early stages the flowers are a mixture of cream, white and pale blue.

Hydrangea macrophylla 'Freudenstein'

'Gartenbaudirektor Kunhert' Producing a dense flat dome head of moderate proportions suitable for cutting, this hydrangea in acidic soils is one of the best blues, having very little white and going straight into sky blue. It also has a tendency to burn in strong sun and so a morsel of shade is appreciated. Sterile florets are clean, smooth-edged and without frills. Not recommended for alkaline soils as the flower color will be muddy. It grows to 5 ft (1.5 m).

'Générale Vicomtesse de Vibraye' Small dense flowerheads of soft cream, almost yellow, gradually turn a shade of the palest sky blue. The individual florets are small, clean and smooth-edged. Certainly one of my favorite hydrangeas, as its delightful shade of powder blue is a rare flower color. (Only 'Mme Truffaut' comes near to this soft blue hue.) It makes a useful cut flower because the heads are not too bulky and so may blend with other blooms. Stems are flecked with wine-red streaks, like a bird's egg. Flowers can burn in the sun and so it needs plenty of moisture or a little shade.

This variety is notable for its reflexed leaves with a tropical drip end. (Tropical plants have a long thin tip to the leaves to shed water much faster than ordinary leaves, which presumably helps them cope with tropical downpours.) These leaves are pale in color but in no way detract from the plant. In fact the light-colored leaves set off the pale blue flowers much better than very dark leaves would. This hydrangea produces lots of flowers per bush and should it lose its terminal flowers to frost, it happily produces more blooms from below. It grows to 5 ft (1.5 m).

'Geoffrey Chadbund' One of the outstanding lacecaps, deserving a place in every garden. The large sterile flowers are spirea-red, turning to rose or magenta in alkaline or slightly acidic soils. It grows to 5 ft (1.5 m).

'Gertrude Glahn' This hydrangea has large heads in a good deep pink, though it becomes purple in acidic soil. It forms a medium-size bush around 5 ft (1.5 m) high and is covered in dense mopheads ideal for cut flowers. A robust healthy variety that always looks good.

'Hamburg' This is one of my favorites. A flowerhead with huge sterile florets, some serrated, some simple

Hydrangea macrophylla 'Geoffrey Chadbund'

33

and some kidney-shaped, yet for all this it presents as a clean bold head of color. In acidic soils it's a superb blue – not royal, not rich, not sky, just plain and simple blue. It maintains this color all through summer, changing to the most incredible wine-red in fall when it is simply stunning as a cut flower. It has good bold dark green leaves and grows to 5 ft (1.5 m).

To increase the size of the heads, prune to reduce the overall number of flowers so the strength is put into a few super-duper blooms.

'Harlequin' This unique hydrangea was known as 'Sensation' for many years. 'Harlequin' has a rounded head of red flowers and each sepal has a frilly white edge or outline, making it a lively two-toned or variegated flower. It's not to everyone's taste, as it is not easy to blend with other shrubs, but it probably has a place as a tub plant near the house. Terraces or patios are probably the best growing situations, as it is rather frost tender. It grows to 3 ft (1 m).

'Heinrich Seidel' (syn 'Glory of Aalsmeer') Large frilly-edged sepals on a good-sized mophead. The heads have a slightly crowded, untidy habit. It forms a tall upright plant to 7 ft (2 m). The flowers are cherry-red in lime soil and are even a good red in slightly acidic soil. It tends to go purple when the soil is very acidic.

'Immaculata' A low-growing dense bush, usually less than 3 ft (1 m). It has very dark rich green foliage. The white florets are brimful, making a very large white mophead. The flowers begin as a delicious shade of cream, then open to pure white. Feed and prune to induce a few enormous heads, or be judicious with the pruning to produce a number of smaller ones. It needs to be grown in shade to prevent burning or sun scorch and makes a brilliant container plant.

Hydrangea macrophylla 'Hamburg'

'Kluis Superba' A somewhat untidy bush that grows to 8 ft (2.5 m) with deep pink or violet-blue flowers, depending on the soil. The colors tend to fade quite quickly. This variety has been superseded by better, more modern hybrids.

'La France' Massive round heads of soft pink to light blue, depending on the acidity of the ground. It forms a tall plant to 7 ft (2 m). It can be reluctant to flower and is best grown in coastal gardens where it is frost free. It is very wind hardy, which is why it is still popular 80 years after being released.

'La Marne' A medium-sized bush (height 5 ft or 1.5 m) with large healthy leaves and huge mopheads

of soft pink or blue, this is a tough, vigorous plant which is ideal for coastal gardens but is also happy inland. It has excellent fall flower colors in smoky pinks, greens and mauves.

'Lanarth White' A pure white lacecap which sometimes tries to be a mophead and so tends to have some intermediate flowers. It has distinctly pointed pale green leaves and forms a compact bush (height 7 ft or 2 m).

This hydrangea's main claim to fame is being the best of the whites for a difficult sunny, dry or coastal site. The flowerheads dry very well, keeping their creamy white color.

Hydrangea macrophylla 'Immaculata'

'Le Cygne' Also known as 'White Swan', a name you may find it under in garden centers, "cygne" being the French name for a cygnet or baby swan. A big tough healthy plant growing to 7 ft (2 m), this hydrangea has white mopheads made up of delightful frilly pointed sepals. Sometimes the heads take on a tinge of pink.

'Libelle' (syns 'Dove', 'Libelle White', 'Dragonfly', 'Snow', 'Teller White') One of the best white lace-caps, it has smooth-edged sepals of pure white that surround the true blue flowers in the middle of the lacecap. The contrast is stunning. The neat flat flowers and the smooth convex leaves create an innocent, wholesome aspect which looks good in formal or informal gardens. It blooms generously all summer until the fall frosts. Sterile sepals are held out nicely and don't crowd the flower. They seem to keep their pristine whiteness longer than other lacecaps, but eventually turn over and take on a pink tinge. Still, there are always new flowers coming on.

The plant is a medium size (5 ft or 1.5 m) and will easily fit in most gardens. Like most of the white lacecaps, it looks superb by water or in a shady situation.

Above: *Hydrangea macrophylla* 'Lilacina'

Right: *Hydrangea macrophylla* 'Libelle'

'Lilacina' Here's a lacecap with a lot of *Hydrangea serrata* blood, judging by the long pointed leaves. The outer sepals are phlox-pink in alkaline soil through to imperial purple in acidic conditions. Internal true flowers are violet and blue. The contrast between the pinky purple and the blue is striking. 'Lilacina' flowers profusely all summer until the frosts begin. It makes an excellent contrast plant because of its upright tidy nature and two-toned flowers. A wonderful shrub for almost any land-scaping purpose, it has the added advantage of being tolerant of the sun. The flowers are exceptional as dried blooms. It grows to 5-7 ft (1.5-2 m).

'Maculata' Sometimes confused with *H.* 'Tricolor' because it has three-colored variegated leaves – green in the center, with patches of gray nearby and a large undefined white edge. It is the large splashes of white that distinguish it from 'Tricolor' and 'Quadricolor'. Despite the latter having more colors, 'Maculata' is the most obviously variegated hydrangea because of the large areas of white in the leaves. It is almost a hosta type of variegation. As a rule, variegated plants either appeal or they don't, but somehow this hydrangea even finds favor with gardeners who usually hate variegated plants. The charming lacecap flowers consist of white to pale pastel mauve sterile florets surrounding rose-purple to violet true flowers, creating a delicate color combination.

This plant has a rather susceptible nature and needs to be in shade to prevent sunburn to the leaves and provide protection from strong winds and frosts. Another flaw is that slugs and snails seem to love it. They can decimate a young plant and possibly kill it. However, it's worth persevering and finding the right spot for this very attractive variety. Try a layer of wood ash around the plant to keep off slugs, give it some shade for protection and it will reward you with a brilliant display of foliage and flowers. It is good for florists too. It grows to 5 ft or 1.5 m.

'Madame Baardse' Bearing lovely round heads of glowing cherry-red on a dense compact plant, this is an early-flowering variety ideal for warm climates. It can be used in tubs and patio planters and grows to 5 ft (1.5 m).

'Madame Emile Mouillère' Buttercream emerging to pure white, modest-sized heads on a medium bush with a slightly lax, very charming habit, this hydrangea is quite different from the dense compact nature of a typical mophead. It can be grown in tubs and pots, though they need to be large to accommodate the lax habit of the bush. The small leaves help to keep the plant in proportion to the pot. It is best in some shade as the flowers tend to burn in full sun or if the plant is too dry at the roots. It takes on a blush-pink tinge in late fall. The florets have very reflexed sepals, forming a dense, almost complete dome. It has clean green stems on a bush that grows to 7 ft (2 m). Feed this variety for large flowers and container culture, for which it is a most popular choice. Ideal in coastal regions because of its glossy leaves, it is more cold hardy than most cultivars. It makes a good beginner's plant as it is easy to grow. In cold climates, it is probably best on a warm sunny wall.

Hydrangea macrophylla 'Masja'

'Madame Faustin Travouillon' (syn 'Peacock') has very pleasing, frilly flat flowers in soft powder-blue, even softer than 'Vibraye'. It has pale leaves and a medium-sized bush (height 5 ft or 1.5 m) and flowerheads. It does well in shade and this helps protect the pale foliage from the heat of the sun. Flowers change to a pleasant shade of green in fall which makes for stunning dried specimens. It is a good variety for container culture.

'Madame Truffaut' has very soft powder-blue flowers on a medium-sized bush (5 ft or 1.5 m). The outer sepals are smooth-edged and clean, with a second double frilled flower within. Florets are frilly-edged or serrated and sit very flat, giving the impression that all four florets are joined into one starry-shaped flower. In early spring the outer sepals are blue while the inner ones are creamy white, which is a delightful contrast.

'Maréchal Foch' This old variety has stood the test of time, being grown for years as one of the best blues, which it is. Even in the pink form it's an attractive plant. Having flowers on both terminal and lateral branches, it is usually smothered in blooms. This habit of flowering on the laterals makes it an ideal plant for cold frosty areas because if the terminal buds are damaged by frost, the later blooming laterals will still produce a crop of flowers. The flowers have a very clean appearance because of the smooth sepals and tight, round heads that dry very successfully. It forms a small to medium-sized shrub (3-7 ft or 1-2 m) suitable for any garden. If it has any faults, they are that the flowers tend to scorch in the sun and it is sometimes attacked by mildew.

'Mariesii' Also known as the Single Large-leaf hydrangea, it has really only been included for historical reasons. This robust lacecap variety was collected in Japan by Charles Maries in 1879 and was used in the early breeding programs. It is the parent of the better garden plants such as 'Blue Wave', 'White Wave', 'Lilacina' and many others. 'Mariesii' itself is floriferous, with a mass of lacecap flowers, though these are often in muddy nondescript shades, unlike its cleaner colored offspring. It can be a good clean soft pink with blue true flowers, or white with just the softest hint of pink and is suitable for most climates. It grows to 7 ft (2 m).

'Masja' A superb dwarf plant dressed in lush healthy dark green leaves and small rounded heads of rich glowing red. A tough hardy hydrangea ideal for any garden situation and perfect for tubs and pots as it has a second burst of flowers late in the season. Released as a cultivar in the 1990s, it is destined to become a popular variety. It grows to 3 ft (1 m).

'Mathilda Gutges' Very rich, dark, black-green foliage, with strongly serrated edges to the rounded leaves, clothe this plant which is almost a dwarf. Modest-sized flowerheads made up of florets that are rounded with serrations at 2-4 and 8-10 o'clock. Phenomenal cobalt-blue flowers are the outstanding feature of this hydrangea, so if space is limited in your garden and you would like a deep rich blue, then this is an excellent choice. It comes into bloom early in the summer and flowers freely. It grows to 3-7 ft (1-2 m).

Hydrangea macrophylla 'Madame Truffaut'

'Merritt's Supreme' (Dark Pink hydrangea) has big, bold heads of dark blue in acidic (pH. 5.5) soil when in full sun. It is a passable blue, although not the best available. However, grow this in shade in a less acidic (pH 6 to 6.5) soil and the effect is remarkable.

The first florets to open are rich lilac, while the newer florets are yellow, eventually turning into a rich maroony purple that seems to glow. In lime soil it forms a superb large head of rosy pink. Florets can be in threes, fours or sixes and are mostly smooth-edged. It has a tendency for one big, one small and two medium florets, which gives it a winged appearance.

The stems have just a few specks of red and the leaves are big and bold in a rich dark green and look good enough to eat. They have serrated edges and a pronounced tropical "drip tip". All this is found on a very compact dense plant which could almost be described as dwarf (3 ft or 1 m) make it ideal for small suburban gardens and for tubs and containers where you can mix and match the colors. The rich metallic-blue fall flowers are glorious when dried.

'Merveille Sanguine' This branch sport of 'Merveille' has the same tough qualities of the parent plant. The flowers are much deeper and richer in color, from blood-red through to wine-purple. "Sanguine" means "blood" and this is certainly one of the richest, darkest reds.

A variety called 'Brunette' is very similar. It grows to 5 ft (1.5 m).

'Miss Belgium' An excellent pink in alkaline soil or in containers. The plant is ideally suited to pot and tub culture as it stays small and compact (3 ft or 1 m) and the rounded heads tend to be tiny, keeping the flowers in proportion to the bush. Its free-flowering habit and healthy nature are its good qualities. It is not the best plant for acidic soils as the flowers will be a strident purple-blue.

'Montgomery' is a small to medium-sized shrub (5 ft or 1.5 m) with masses of fairly small heads. In an acidic soil the purple-magenta flowers have a blue luster in the center which has your retina vibrating. The flowers can vary from rich ruby-red in alkaline soil to beet-purple and maroon in strongly acidic

gardens. Clean, flat flowers give the impression of being fused to form complete circles of sepals, which turn exciting red and purple colors when fall arrives. It is reasonably sun tolerant.

'Mousseline' A very unusual-looking mophead hydrangea. The pale blue flowers look like they have been stroked like a cat, as all the sepals are curved back to give a smooth outline to the head instead of the usual cup-shaped florets. The rounded smooth outline of the sepals adds to this clean, uniform appearance. It reaches 6 ft (1.8 m) and can be grown in full sun or part shade and the flowers change to pale green late in the season.

'Nightingale' (syn 'Nachtigall') Simply stunning – to my mind this is the best blue lacecap. It is a tall upright shrub with very dark foliage. Nicely presented lacecaps in rich cornflower blue are shown off to their best against a background of healthy dark green leaves.

The large sterile sepals are simple and true, smooth-edged with just a hint of white when they open. If it has one fault, it's not frost hardy in every region, otherwise it knocks the socks off

Hydrangea macrophylla 'Montgomery'

'Blue Wave' and 'Mariesii'. It is a very clean, disease-free hydrangea and ideal for warmer coastal climates. It grows to 5 ft (1.5 m).

'Nigra' (syn 'Mandschurica') A Chinese cultivar imported by Ernest Wilson as *Hydrangea mandschurica*, a name which is sometimes still used. This variety has one major claim to fame – its shiny black stems.

The small rounded mopheads range from delicate pink to soft blue, depending on the soil. They can be a muddy color in neutral soil and a harsh purple in very acidic soil. If grown vigorously to ensure strong black stems, then it has some garden merit. It grows to 5 ft (1.5 m).

'Nikko Blue' If you want a small bush covered in tight blue heads, then 'Nikko Blue' is for you. It is covered in neat round heads of striking blue in acidic soils, and is best ignored if your soil is alkaline. It is probably happiest in slight shade, and can be a little slow to establish, otherwise it is highly recommended. It forms a modest-sized bush of 5 ft (1.5 m).

Hydrangea macrophylla 'Nigra'

'Otaksa' An old Japanese cultivar named by Philipp von Siebold after a Japanese girl, this forms a big bold plant to 8 ft (2.5 m) with huge flowerheads. The enormous creamy flowers have the faintest shade of flax blue in acidic soils and the softest hint of pink in alkaline ones. Although considered out of fashion, this variety still has some attributes we can utilize. It has shiny glossy leaves like 'Ayesha' and 'Seafoam' and is probably just a mophead form of the wild macrophylla. Like 'Ayesha', it is frost tender. The shiny leaves signify it is very wind tolerant and ideal for coastal gardens. The flowers turn the palest shade of green in fall and are perfect for drying.

'Parzifal' If constancy is your motto, then pass on to the next entry, but if you think variety is the spice of life, then 'Parzifal' is for you. The small tight round head is made up of very frilly serrated florets which overlap and create a starry appearance. This exciting and unusual plant often bears three different colored heads at the one time. In acidic soil it is common to see pink, magenta-rose and light sea-blue flowers all on the one bush. In fall the colors change to rose and purples. A smallish flowerhead makes this the perfect plant for cut flowers and dried material. Its modest bush size (to 5 ft or 1.5 m) and variable colors also make it very suitable for small gardens. It is probably best in slight shade to protect the colors from burning and to maintain flower quality for later cutting. It is ideal in any soil.

'Pia' (syn 'Piamina', 'Winning Edge', 'Pink Elf', Dwarf hydrangea) This is a very distinct variety. It is a truly dwarf plant, rarely exceeding 2 ft (60 cm). Usually a pink to pale red in alkaline soil, it is an excellent border edging subject for these conditions and is also outstanding as a windowbox or tub plant when it can be kept pink. It blooms in a pleasing mauve in neutral soil but becomes rather harsh in acidic conditions.

'Princess Beatrix' Very pointed distinctly serrate huge sterile florets in threes, fours or fives help to form this dense, broad mophead. The color is a superb soft pink with a hint of brown changing to soft magenta-rose. One of the best pinks for an acidic soil, 'Princess Beatrix' is a low-growing bush (5 ft or 1.5 m) with healthy foliage and distinct spots and lines on the stems.

'Quadricolor' (syn 'Yellow Wave', 'Lemon Wave') This unusual variety has four distinct leaf colors: two shades of green (light and dark) creamy white and vivid yellow. The strong yellow color is on the edges of most of the leaves and is the easy way to tell *H.* 'Quadricolor' from the other variegated hydrangeas, 'Maculata' and 'Tricolor'.

The lacecaps are white to very pale pink or blue. A popular plant with flower arrangers because of the very different variegated foliage, it is also sought after by slugs and snails, so be warned! It needs shade to prevent sun-scorch to the leaves. It grows to 5 ft (1.5 m).

'Red Emperor' If you want to grow a good red and your soil is acidic then this could be the variety for you. It forms a good dense shrub from 4-5 ft (1-1.5 m). Small tidy heads of rosy-red flowers abound, even in very acidic soil. In alkaline ground it is a vivid crimson, whereas acidic conditions turn it to ruby-red and even magnolia-purple. Whatever the soil, you'll be pleased with the result.

'Red Star' A wonderful variety that vividly demonstrates the hydrangea's flower color changeability. Usually described as a good round-headed red flower, this turns to an incredibly rich French blue in acidic soils, which makes a nonsense of its name.

'Rotschwanz' (syn 'Redstart') This is a magnificent new Teller lacecap, whose ray florets are long and fluted with a slight twist – propeller fashion. It has distinctly two-toned white and red true flowers and

Hydrangea macrophylla 'Princess Beatrix'

takes on wine-red colors in the fall. A tough robust healthy shrub which is highly recommended, it grows to 4 ft (1.2 m).

'Schenkenberg' You will enjoy the beautiful cherry-red mophead flowers on this tidy compact bush. This variety is ideally suited to containers and tubs where the pH can be controlled to keep the flowers red. Containers also suit its compact habit, it grows to 3 ft (1 m), and free-flowering nature.

Hydrangea macrophylla 'Quadricolor'

Above: *Hydrangea macrophylla* 'Red Emperor'

Above right: *Hydrangea macrophylla* 'Seafoam'

'Seafoam' Thought by some to be the wild form of *Hydrangea macrophylla*, this is sometimes called *H. maritima* 'Seafoam', the "maritima" referring to the maritime or coastal habit of the original wild hydrangeas. As the name suggests, 'Seafoam' is quite happy growing near the sea and has large glossy leaves which seem to cope quite happily with the littoral.

The bold lacecap flowers, pleasantly scented, can be 1 ft (30 cm) wide. Large white sterile florets surround the mass of lilac-mauve to blue fertile flowers. This tall plant will grow to 7 ft (2 m) and tolerates full sun, shade and wind, including salt wind.

'Sir Joseph Banks' is a vigorous old-fashioned variety with large mopheads of white or the palest pink/blue, depending on the soil. It grows happily near the sea and tolerates the fiercest of gales. It is prone to frost damage inland, so is best grown in temperate regions. The frosts may kill off the emerging flowerbuds or severely damage the plant. It is really only of value as a backdrop or for windy sites. It grows to 10 ft (3 m).

'Sister Thérèse' (syn 'Soeur Thérèse') This was originally called 'Petite Soeur Thérèse de 'Enfant Jésus'. It is a lovely pure white mophead that grows to perfection in the shade. The flowers tend to scorch in the sun. It has a rather lax open habit because the weight of the flowers tends to bow the stems, but this adds to the charm of the plant. It grows to 7 ft (2 m). The flowers take on a pleasant pink tinge in fall.

'Sontagskind' Sometimes known as 'Sunday's Child', which is the English translation, this is an excellent new dark-red cultivar. Nice tight round heads are well presented above a small bush (3 ft or 1 m). It's hardy and easy to grow in any region and is destined to become one of the standard red varieties.

'Souvenir du Président Doumer' On a bush with small dark rounded serrated leaves and spotty stems, clean smooth-edged sepals form neat round heads. As the season rolls on these superb reddish and light maroon fist-sized heads gradually intensify in color to become ruby-red or crimson so that the bush positively sings of summer. This hydrangea offers splendid colors in any soil, but has a slightly weak constitution, performing best in warm climates. It grows to 4 ft (1.2 m).

'Taube' Rich pink lacecap flowers are seen above strong healthy foliage on this hydrangea, though it does tend to go blue in acidic soil. It is one of the many new Teller hybrids from Switzerland. Most of the Teller hydrangeas are named after birds and this one is no exception – "taube" translates as "pigeon". It is happy growing in shade and will reach 5 ft (1.5 m).

'Tokyo Delight' On this variety, pure white sepals surround the soft pink, true flowers in a small lacecap fashion. These two-toned flowers are presented in tiers, making it a hydrangea hard to resist. It forms a fairly robust, upright bush to 7 ft (2 m). The heads gradually turn pink and eventually a red color. It is one of the few hydrangeas to have colored leaves in fall.

'Tovelit' This dwarf plant is ideal for pots and tubs, or for planting at the front of a border. It rarely grows above 3 ft (1 m) high and its bright pink heads turn purple-mauve in acidic soil. The sepals are pointed and look like Christmas stars drawn by children. The heads are crowded with flowers all trying to show off their stars, thus forming a unique cluttered appearance.

'Tosca' Shaded from lovely pale pink to soft lilac, this variety's mopheads have a number of double flowers with a serrated edge. It is a strong plant, with a good constitution and is worth growing for its unusual flower color.

'Tricolor' This has deep green, grayish green and pale yellow foliage. White sterile flowers have a tinge of pink in a lacecap shape. It is believed to be a sport of *H.m.* 'Mariesii'. Slugs and snails will devastate the plant if it's not protected, and it needs shade. It grows to 7 ft (2 m).

'Veitchii' This Japanese variety was taken to England by Charles Maries for his employer, the Veitch Nursery. It grows 7 ft (2 m) high and can form a wide-spreading robust shrub.

The big flat white lacecaps have the sterile sepals in threes, which is unusual, as they are usually in fours. The flowers take on a pink and then red tinge as the summer drifts on.

Slugs and snails are fans of this variety, which has healthy-looking foliage. 'Veitchii' has stood the test of time but there are now better white lacecaps available, such as 'Libelle', 'White Wave' and 'Tokyo Delight'.

'White Wave' is a sister plant to 'Blue Wave' and 'Lilacina', as all of them are seedlings of *H.m.* 'Mariesii'. All the superb lacecap flowers bloom pure white initially, then the true flowers tend to take on a pinky mauve tinge as the summer glides on, while the sterile flowers turn over in typical fashion and change to pink.

A good strong plant, 5 ft (1.5 m) high, or occasionally up to 7 ft (2 m), 'White Wave' is happy in sun or shade, though in a colder climate it tends to flower better in full sun. It really lights up a dark shady corner.

Hydrangea macrophylla 'Tosca'

'Zaunkönig' (syn 'Wren') The name of this Swiss Teller hybrid means "wren", a tiny European bird that makes a domed nest. The flat medium-sized lacecap flowers are deep vivid erythrocyte red in alkaline conditions, or rich sea-lavender violet in acidic soils. Scalloped sterile sepals surround the pinky-mauve true flowers and some of the sterile florets are raised above the lacecap, giving a two-tiered effect. It is best in a warm climate and grows to 5 ft (1.5 m).

Hydrangea serrata forms

Hydrangea serrata is hardy to Zone 6. It is reasonably tolerant of frosts but is not happy in coastal gardens, windy sites or full sun.

'Blue Bird' is a small bush with shapely lacecaps of pale blue. The sepals are distinctly rounded and arranged in a cross fashion, the dome of true flowers within is a slightly richer blue. The tidy structure of the flower adds to the charm of this serrata hybrid, which is hard to beat for color, long flowering season, hardiness and grace. Just to top it off, 'Blue Bird' is one of the few hydrangeas with fall leaf color, turning red in late summer. It grows to 4 ft (1.2 m) and is best in some shade. Some people say this is the same as *Hydrangea serrata acuminata*, but having grown *H.s. acuminata* from wild collected seed, I'm convinced they are different.

'Blue Deckle' Here's a delightful little plant which forms a bush to just 2 ft (60 cm) and so is ideally suited to small gardens and pots. However, it can be just as beautiful as a drift of plants in a bigger garden. Very large deckle-edged sepals in soft powder-blue surround and almost mound the pale blue true flowers.

The overall effect is of a small mound of flowers rather than a lacecap. It can be soft smoky pink in soils over pH 6.

This variety was raised by Michael Haworth-Booth, a great plantsman and hydrangea fanatic. It would grace any small garden and probably looks loveliest with just a hint of shade.

'Grayswood' This is a gem. A pretty, delicate-looking plant, appearances are deceptive as it is quite robust and frost hardy. The shrub grows to 5 ft (1.5 m). It has intriguing spotty stems, but the highlight is its white lacecaps that change to soft pink, then a rose color and finally the color of red wine. The plant needs sunlight to encourage all these color changes, and the bush can exhibit a multitude of colors at any one time.

'Impératrice Eugénie' On this bush the dainty little mophead flowers begin a creamy yellow before opening to pure white. Gradually the flowers take on a pink tinge, becoming richer in color as the summer progresses, until finally the flowers are a vibrant red-wine color. Have a care to find the spot for this hydrangea so it performs at its best. In too much shade the flowers are reluctant to change color, as it is the action of the sunshine that encourages the variation. If you plant it in too hot and dry a spot, the flowers will burn or scorch. Ideally you need a place which receives sun for half of the day and is moist enough to prevent sun scorch. The flowers are so fantastic it is definitely worth the extra effort to grow this to perfection. It grows to 4 ft (1.3 m).

'Kiyosumi' This plant is my new favorite hydrangea. Found on Mount Kiyosumi in Japan in the 1950s, it will almost certainly become a favorite in North American gardens. Everything about it is so different. The narrow pointed leaves have a reddish tinge, sometimes taking on a burgundy hue. Then, when the pink lacecap flowers first form on top of the bush you think it is nothing special, that is until the outer sterile flowers open up. The white flowers are edged in red! This eye-catching bush can be grown in pots and tubs, or in a slightly shady part of the garden.

Above: *Hydrangea macrophylla* 'Grayswood'
Left: *Hydrangea macrophylla* 'Zaunkönig'

'Miranda' Every gardener should be able to find a spot for this little gem, a wonderful plant ideal for any soil and superb in containers. Its dwarf nature is an advantage, for it grows to only 24 in (60 cm) high. The leaves are long, pointy and rather pale, and the little lacecap flowers sit up proudly above the foliage. The sterile florets are very smooth and rounded. They help give the flat lacecap a clean and pure appearance. In an alkaline soil the flower is soft flesh-pink, whereas in acidic ground it is a superb rich dark butterfly-blue. It tends to look muddy in neutral soils, and has two other faults: it needs

45

coddling for a year or two to get established, and the flower season is fairly short.

'Preziosa' ('Preciosa', Sawtooth hydrangea) One out of the box. A real treat for any garden, 'Preziosa' is constantly changing color. It progresses from white to pink to red and finally wine-red come fall. Actually the many changes are even more dramatic if followed from the beginning of summer. The small heads open green, quickly changing to yellow, then cream and finally white before developing pink tinges and spots, becoming totally pink and then red, a delicious red so different to macrophylla reds. Finally it turns maroon to wine-red. The added bonus is that all these color changes happen regardless of the soil pH and so everyone can achieve the same result. (Note, however, that it can go a slightly inky color in very acidic conditions.)

This hydrangea tolerates wet soil and needs slight shade to perform at its best, for it tends to burn or scorch if sited in too sunny or too dry a spot. 'Preziosa' forms an upright shrub, 5 ft (1.5 m) high, with distinct reddish stems and slightly red-hued leaves. Fairly small flowerheads sit up proud on top of the plant. The sepals are slightly frilled or deckled with net veining, and the stems are rather thin and delicate. Imagine this delightful shrub in flower for

Above and opposite top: *Hydrangea serrata* 'Preziosa'
Opposite bottom: *Hydrangea serrata* 'Miranda'

four to five months progressing through five color changes and adapting to most situations. Given a little shade, a good mulch and fed regularly, this hydrangea will delight you for longer than any other plant in your garden.

CHAPTER 4

Rare Hydrangeas and Hydrangea Relatives

Rare hydrangeas

Hydrangea serrata chinensis

This rare small 3 ft (1 m) shrub with dark green foliage comes from southeast China and Taiwan. The hard shiny leaves have a serrated edge. It tends to be evergreen in a warm climate. The delightful white lacecaps show up splendidly against the dark foliage. Happy in sun or shade, it needs a warm spot in a colder climate and is probably only hardy to Zone 7.

Hydrangea indochinensis

Hydrangea indochinensis

Several forms of this frost tender species have been collected in Vietnam and China in recent years. They vary from an upright form with shiny dark green pointed leaves with a purple reverse to rounded bushes more like *H. chinensis*. The flowers are white to pale lilac lacecaps. It is probably only hardy to Zone 9.

Hydrangea involucrata

A small shrub (3 ft or 1 m) with pretty mauve-colored true flowers surrounded by a few white sterile florets. The leaves are rather rough to the touch. Not a particularly frost hardy shrub (hardy to Zone 7) and not easy to grow well, this is a collector's piece from Japan and Taiwan.

Hydrangea involucrata 'Hortensis'

Bearing showy heads of double flowers in the palest opaque pink, this small shrub (height 3 ft or 1 m) has a poor constitution and is therefore difficult to grow. It is hardy to Zone 7. It is, however, worth persevering with for the lovely flowers.

Some interesting relatives

Decumaria barbara

A semi-evergreen climber from the southern Appalachian Mountains, this has clinging roots like climbing hydrangeas. Like them, it will grow in shade but tends to flower better if given some sunlight. It has corymbs of white all-true flowers. It is hardy to Zone 8.

Decumaria sinensis

Also known as wood vamp, this Chinese version of *Decumaria* is truly evergreen. Its small white flowers in early summer are deliciously scented. It is hardy to Zone 8.

Dichroa versicolor

An unusual evergreen relative of the hydrangea, this is originally from North Burma and a recent introduction to cultivation. It forms a bold shrub with large glossy leaves, very similar in shape and size to those of *Hydrangea macrophylla* but a richer, darker green. It has an upright form, growing 7 ft (2 m) high and a little less wide. The overall effect is a tropical-looking plant, and yet it is proving quite frost hardy in my Zone 9 garden, surviving frosts over several winters if given a little shade and shelter. The kind of late frosts that ruin the flowerbuds of magnolias and rhododendrons leave this shrub untouched. However, the best is still to come – the rich denim-blue flowers are produced more or less all year round.

Dichroa versicolor is a simply stunning plant that I'm sure will become very popular in time. It will grow at the water's edge, tolerating quite wet conditions, and also contends with shade and even drought, although it does not do the plant credit when conditions are too dry. It seems the flower color is unaffected by acidity, unlike its hydrangea relatives.

Other *Dichroa* species include *D. febrifuga* from Nepal and *D. hirsuta* from Vietnam, with smaller, narrow leaves and small heads of pinkish or blue flowers. Their intense blue berries last long into winter, but compared to *D. versicolor* these other species are of only passing interest. *Dichroa* species are generally hardy to Zone 8.

Pileostegia viburnoides

An evergreen climber that ascends using sucker roots to cling to tree trunks and walls, etc. The thick fleshy dark green pointed leaves are very handsome and it's worth being patient with this slow-growing climber as in time it will reward you with not only

Above: *Dichroa versicolor*
Below: *Pileostegia viburnoides*

lush foliage but also heads of frothy, creamy white flowers. It will grow in difficult shady places as long as the soil is rich and well-drained. One of the very few frost hardy evergreen climbers, it was introduced by E.H. Wilson in 1908, from Khasia Hills, India. It is hardy to Zone 9.

CHAPTER 5

The Special Qualities
of Garden Hydrangeas

The mainstay of the summer garden

Covered with flowers for months at a time, hydrangeas are the mainstay of any summer garden. The bees can't work their magic on hydrangeas' sterile flowers. Without the effort needed to produce seeds, these plants merrily flower for months and months. With the possible exception of hybrid roses, no other shrub flowers for so long a period as hydrangeas.

Some gardeners scoff at the ease with which hydrangeas can be grown. Don't listen to them – they are missing out on a wonderful array of color, form and style in the summer and fall garden. Personally, I wish every plant was as easy to grow as a hydrangea. If you want a challenge, then find some new or remarkable way of displaying these shrubs so they look even more beautiful.

Color all the way

Everyone wants color in their summer garden and the hydrangeas are screaming "here I am". Most shrubs are spring-flowering to ensure they have a warm summer period in which to produce their seeds. There is a scarcity of summer-flowering shrubs. Roses, hibiscus, cistus and the subshrub penstemon are all summer-flowering, and of these only the rose is reliably frost hardy. All four insist on being in a sunny site, whereas hydrangeas will grow in sun or shade and have the huge advantage of blending easily with far more of the summer-flowering herbaceous plants. Roses are notoriously difficult to blend with other plants. Hibiscus tend to

Above: Fall flower colors.

Opposite: *Hydrangea macrophylla* 'Blue Prince'

dominate any scene they feature in, and need a lot of summer heat to thrive. Cistus are short-lived and penstemons need mild winters, so to my mind hydrangeas are the clear winners in the summer-flowering stakes.

Fall color is just as desirable in the shrub garden. Many of the *H. macrophylla* and *H. serrata* flowers change color as the season progresses and this adds a whole new dimension to the garden. Imagine a group of rich blue summer flowers transformed into a rich wine-red color, breathing new life into the fall

Hydrangea macrophylla 'Hamburg' in summer.

landscape. Many of the whites, including *H. paniculata* and *H. quercifolia*, take on a pink tinge in fall, and some of the *serrata* types go on to develop rich red colors. Fall flower colors in hydrangeas can vary from pale greens and rosy mauve through to rich burgundy and magenta. As well as blending supremely well with the fall tints of the surrounding trees and shrubs, hydrangeas bring the rich colors to ground level.

Hydrangeas are not widely recognized for fall leaf color, with one notable exception. *H. quercifolia* cultivars have stupendous rich burgundy and purple leaves late in the season, and they hold this color for several weeks.

Color change and variability give hydrangeas their unique charm. Summer flowers of hydrangea bloom in a range of colors, including white, pink, red and blue. Blue is irresistible to gardeners, for it is such a scarce commodity. Hydrangeas could be described as the chameleons of the plant world. Many of the mophead types change color according to the acidity of the soil they are planted in. No other plant is capable of doing this, and hydrangeas

provide a wonderful opportunity for us to be creative and mix and match our own colors. As we have seen, these shrubs change their flower color through the season and thus provide a different image in fall. With careful selection we can present a fabulous range of colors to complement the changing garden scene.

Some regard this color change as an impediment to garden design. If you want to live in a world where everything is perfect and life is constant, then probably hydrangeas are not for you, but if you have a generous and creative nature, then these plants will suit your artistic temperament. The fact that hydrangeas are so easy to grow also allows you to be more creative with color and form.

The most versatile of shrubs

Hydrangeas are incredibly versatile plants that will grow in myriad situations. Their ability to thrive in sun or shade means you can use them in many of your garden's difficult sites. There is a hydrangea to suit more or less any position in the garden, for they are tough, resilient plants and generally not fussy about soil or site.

While generally regarded as shade-lovers, most hydrangeas will happily grow in sun if the ground is moist enough. They will even grow in hot and dry places, but the flower quality will suffer because the large leaves and flowerheads need lots of moisture to sustain them. In too dry a spot the flowers will scorch and burn and so the flower show is ruined for that summer. *H. paniculata* is more tolerant of sunny dry sites because of its smaller leaves, and among the macrophylla types, generally the lacecaps will tolerate drier conditions than the mopheads, as they have fewer flowers to keep filled with moisture.

H. macrophylla types are very tolerant of many conditions that would bring about the demise of lesser plants. For instance, they will contend with shade as long as the soil is moist enough and the shade is not from big dense evergreen or coniferous plants. Shade often means the soil is dry, which can

be more of a problem than the lack of sun. All hydrangeas will tolerate some shade if it is not too dense or dry. Certainly they can put up with more shade than most popular shrubs. Some of the lacecaps and mopheads look showier when grown in shade and it may be essential to grow them there if you have very cold winters, when the canopy will protect the plants from the worst of the frosts.

Hydrangeas are not too fussy about the condition of the soil, while fibrous-rooted plants such as rhododendrons are fastidious. The resilient hydrangea will grow in clay, stony and even sandy soil, as long as there is enough moisture. The big-leaved *H. macrophylla* will also tolerate quite wet soil conditions, certainly more so than most garden shrubs.

This adaptability allows us to utilize wet and even marshy ground. Likewise, this ability to grow in moist soils allows us to plant hydrangea shrubs along stream banks and pond edges where we are usually restricted to growing only perennials. In such situations we see again how forgiving hydrangeas are. Since *H. macrophylla* has such bold leaves it blends superbly with moisture-loving hostas.

The ability to grow happily in either acidic or alkaline (limy) soils is another major attribute of these plants. Most other shrubs will not perform well in alkaline areas. Plants such as rhododendrons and camellias insist on acidic soil or they will die. Lilac or syringa is one of the few shrubs apart from hydrangea to actually like lime soil. This soil allows us to grow wonderful pink and red varieties of *H. macrophylla*. Other hydrangea species will also tolerate lime or alkaline soils.

If hydrangeas have a fault, it is that they are so forgiving of the conditions we inflict on them that we sometimes see poor bedraggled specimens surviving on hot, dry clay banks. Any other shrub,

Top, middle and bottom left: *Hydrangea macrophylla* 'Merritt's Supreme' changes color in different soil acidity, from pink in pH 7 to blue in pH 5.

such as a rose or rhododendron, in the same situation would have succumbed to the elements in the first year.

Easy-care, fuss-free, affordable plants

Hydrangeas are easy plants to grow and this is a blessing for new gardeners. They need no coddling like a rhododendron or rose. Once planted, hydrangeas demand very little attention. Even if you never touched them again, they would most likely thrive and put on a fantastic show every summer. If you want them to give of their best, then a deep mulch of bark and an occasional feed would help. They will perform better and exceed your expectations if you give them favorable and kindly treatment. You can prune the macrophylla and paniculata types every winter, but they'll forgive you if you forget, and will still flower for you the next summer. And what's more, the pruning is easy – nothing complex here, and no thorns!

If you decide you've planted your hydrangeas in the wrong place, they can be very easily shifted to a different site within your garden if you want to remedy the problem. This is because they have a large mat of fibrous roots near the soil surface and so when shifted their root volume is not reduced too much. Other shrubs with stringy or widespread root systems often die after being transplanted. Winter or early spring is the ideal time to dig up and transplant hydrangeas. Take care when moving old entrenched hydrangeas, as they will have a firm grip on the ground. (It may be easier to buy or propagate another plant rather than try to transplant a big established specimen.)

Hydrangeas are easily affordable compared to most other shrubs. This is because they are relatively easy to propagate. Only the new cultivars have a scarcity value and therefore a higher price. Once you have established favorites, it is rewarding to propagate new plants from your own cuttings, and the process is not at all difficult. (See Chapter 11.)

Hydrangeas growing in shade. *Hydrangea serrata* at the front, *H. s.* 'Impèratrice Eugènie' is the white and *Hydrangea macrophylla* 'Heinrich Seidel' at the back.

Hydrangeas are relatively free of pests and diseases. It's quite likely you will never need to spray your hydrangea for insects or diseases from the day you plant it until the day you die. (Hydrangeas are also very long-lasting shrubs, as well as being healthy, so they will quite likely outlive you and me both!)

Hydrangeas, especially *H. macrophylla* types, are great weed suppressors. They are tall enough and dense enough to block out the light and prevent weeds getting established. Light is the vital factor for weeds to get started and if the ground is kept covered with either foliage or mulch, or both, the weeds don't stand a chance.

Climbing hydrangeas add a new dimension to the garden

Climbing varieties also help confirm the versatility of the hydrangea genus. Climbing hydrangeas and their close relative, *Schizophragma*, can be grown in full sun, in shade, or from a shady base into

Schizophragma hydrangeoides grown as a climber to hide a shed.

sunshine. In other words, they are one of the easiest climbers to please, and add a new dimension to the late-summer garden.

Climbing hydrangeas, including *Schizophragma*, are valuable for covering walls, unsightly fences and small utility structures. They can even be used as a ground cover. They are brilliant for covering old tree stumps and of course they will happily grow up a live trunk so long as the tree does not have peeling bark. (Trees with this habit shed the climbing roots along with their bark and so they're difficult for a climber to colonize.)

Like ivy, these hydrangeas use roots to cling to whatever you give them. If you want to disguise an old shed or water tank or hide some garden monstrosity, then climbing hydrangeas are a perfect solution. Why not try something original? Send a climbing hydrangea up a utility pole.

Pileostegia and *Decumaria* are less well-known climbers in the hydrangea family. They are covered in more detail in Chapter 4. These evergreen frost hardy climbers deserve to be more popular, for such plants are a scarce commodity.

Be patient with climbing hydrangeas as they are not inclined to romp and take over, as many other climbers do. They may need a few years to get established and to develop the side growths that produce the flowers. In the long run this is an advantage, as you will not need to be pruning the plant every year. Usually only very occasional pruning is needed to shape the plant, e.g. around windows, if necessary.

Decorative in both house and garden . . .

Many hydrangeas are ideally suited for container cultivation, especially the smaller-growing varieties. Both *H. macrophylla* and *H. quercifolia* look wonderful in tubs or large pots. The smaller varieties of *H. macrophylla* are very popular as indoor pot plants because of their long flowering season. In both cases they need lots of water and feeding to be at their best. These same varieties can be forced into flower at different seasons when grown as indoor pot plants. (More about growing hydrangeas in containers in Chapter 12.)

Hydrangeas provide wonderful cut flowers. This is especially true of the *H. macrophylla* types. Some of the showy forms of *H. paniculata* and *H. quercifolia* are equally good for floral art. These same flowers can be cut and dried for winter decoration as dried heads. (See Chapter 12 for details.)

. . . and fragrant too

As a final bonus, some of these versatile hydrangeas have scented flowers. Many of the lacecap varieties and some of the species plants have a pleasant spring fragrance. *Hydrangea macrophylla* 'Seafoam' and *H. arborescens* are especially fragrant. *Hydrangea paniculata* is strongly scented (a little too strong for some tastes).

You can now see how easy it is to please hydrangeas, and how adaptable and versatile they are. There is bound to be a hydrangea to suit more or less any position in your garden.

CHAPTER 6

Landscaping with Hydrangeas

Garden frontages and entrances, driveways and house borders

Let's start at the gate. A group of hydrangeas at the front gate makes a bold summer statement. Their long flowering season ensures they will be a focal point for many months. Hydrangeas are bold dense plants ideal for a spot next to the gate or a path. You can use their strong shapes to add stability to a scene and they can be used to clearly delineate a pathway or entrance. They are impressive shrubs to line the path to the house or border the driveway if you are lucky enough to have a long drive.

Hydrangeas perform well in areas that require low maintenance and little effort. For instance, a group of mopheads planted along a road frontage presents glorious color to the passers-by all summer. Even in tough sites, like those of holiday houses where you may only live for a few weeks of the year and so do not have a chance to cultivate a garden, hydrangeas would be a good choice. Likewise, when you need a plant for a memorial, say in a cemetery, a colorful and resilient hydrangea will fit the bill.

Hydrangeas have the ability to blend into both formal and informal gardens. Formal areas near the house are perfect sites for mophead varieties. Their compact habit and rounded heads seem somehow to "ground" the walls. These dense shrubs also help suppress the weeds and enable you to be a relaxed gardener in the hotter months.

Another bonus is finding varieties that will easily

Opposite: Hydrangeas at an entranceway with a traditional white picket fence.

fit under windows without threatening to block out the sunlight. As hydrangeas are deciduous and easily pruned, you can readily access buildings and services if ever you need to paint walls, windows, etc. The plants will even tolerate being pruned in summer if that is essential, though it's not recommended.

There are varieties best suited to the sunny side of the house, e.g. the macrophyllas 'Altona', 'Gentian Dome', 'Merrit's Supreme' and 'Souvenir du Président Doumer'. Those most successful on the shady side are the whites or soft pinks and blues.

Growing hydrangeas in tubs and raised borders around the house is another popular way of utilizing these charming shrubs. There is something inherently formal about the round mophead flowers even though the bushes can be rather lax in their habit due to their rapid growth. Hydrangeas are glorious in formal gardens, perhaps behind boxwood hedges, and the ideal choice where matching pairs of plants are required. Because they grow rapidly each season, any two plants can be made to look identical in a short period of time. Hydrangeas have long been popular in the extremely formal gardens of Portugal and France because of their habit of even growth and generally formal nature.

A big bold group of mopheads at the end of a lawn makes an impressive sight. The contrast of green lawn with the rounded dense plants and showy flowers is simple and effective – and what is more, it is a long-lasting display.

Hydrangea paniculata 'Grandiflora' can be used in much the same way as the mophead hydrangeas. It is best in full sun. Beside the house or along a driveway groups of these shrubs provide stunning late-summer flowers. Their magnificent conical heads of white suit a formal setting. There are various forms of *H. paniculata*, from the larger-growing *H.p.* 'Floribunda', best featured in an informal garden, to the smaller-growing 'Kyushu' with its lacy flowers. This variety fits easily in any small garden, and is equally successful in a formal or informal design.

Hydrangea quercifolia and its forms can be a bit tricky to grow in a cold climate. The plant itself will grow and survive in regions with quite cold winters, say up to Zone 5, and yet it only performs and flowers well in areas with warm summers. If you live in a cool region you may need to plant it in a hot spot in sun near the house. Again, these hydrangeas can be used in settings similar to those recommended for the mopheads – by the gate, along paths, near house walls.

Herbaceous and mixed borders

The hydrangea's habit of flowering in summer is just one of its many landscaping qualities. It allows us to grow the shrubs as companion plants in a herbaceous border. Both the flowers and the leaves of hydrangeas will combine perfectly with perennial plants. Mopheads and lacecaps both blend easily with cottage-garden designs.

Plants of *Hydrangea macrophylla* are fine at the front or in the middle of a border, while the lacecaps will probably look better at the back. The lacecap flowers are so dainty they give the appearance of butterflies gathering on a bush, a light and fluffy effect very appropriate to the season.

Hydrangea aspera and the taller forms of *H. paniculata* look splendid at the back of a herbaceous border. The best of the species for smaller gardens would be *H. aspera* var *villosa*, which has superb two-toned pink and mauve lacecap flowers in late summer and makes a perfect border backdrop.

While many shrubs look out of place in a herbaceous border, the hydrangeas sit quite happily. Some other popular shrubs are unsuitable for a perennial border as they are either spring-flowering

Hydrangeas in a herbaceous border. 'Red Emperor' at front, with 'Montgomery' behind the agapanthus.

and therefore not compatible or their foliage is too bold and dark, as is the case with rhododendrons.

Hydrangea macrophylla and *H. serrata*, with a range of white to soft pink, reds, mauve and blue mophead or lacecap flowers and heights varying from 2 ft (60 cm) to 10 ft (3 m), give the landscaper endless possibilities for blending hydrangeas with other shrubs and perennials. To give just one example: intermingled with rhododendrons and camellias, hydrangeas lighten the dark evergreen effect while repeating the rounded bush theme. Being deciduous, hydrangeas change the pattern just enough to break the monotony of round dense dark plants.

In a temperate garden, *Camellia japonica* will provide winter color, leading to the spring flush of rhododendrons, followed by the summer-long hydrangea flowers which, as they change into fall

Above: *Hydrangea macrophylla* 'Mathilda Gutges' in a
mixed border.
Left: Hydrangeas in a mixed border with rhododendrons
and perennials.

mode, will be superseded by the dainty blossom of
the early flowering *Camellia sasanqua*. Thus you can
have all-year color for not much effort, as all three
are low-maintenance plants if mulched well.

Woodland gardens

The happy combination of rhododendrons and
azaleas with hydrangeas in a woodland garden
extends the season of interest beyond the usual
spring display. These plants also add a light, airy feel
to a woodland scene. They bring drama to some
shady sites where most other flowering shrubs would
fade away. In bold groups under the shade of big
trees they are equally successful, or planted in drifts
alongside paths or down banks. White lacecaps are
especially attractive in woodland settings and will

Above: *Hydrangea macrophylla* 'Libelle' with the trunks of silver birch behind.

Above: Hydrangeas are tough plants, suitable for children's play areas.

bring dark areas to life. White is a wonderful color to brighten up a shady spot and the white hydrangeas do better in shade as the flowers will not scorch.

Stream- and lakeside locations are fine for *H. macrophylla* types as they tolerate wet or moist ground. Normally only perennials grow so close to water and having a shrub that is happy in this situation gives the garden designer more flexibility. Bold mopheads can be used to good effect where the expanse of water is big enough to provide reflections. In general, the other hydrangea species are not happy in wet soil and need to be planted in free-draining areas away from the water.

Parks, schools and industrial parks

Spring-flowering shrubs are common in parks and gardens, yet spring is a season of low visitor numbers because of the cool weather. People visit parks in summer when the weather is more inviting, and I believe city parks departments could make much better use of low-maintenance hydrangeas for simple and effective color in warmer months.

Hydrangeas can be grown in herbaceous borders and are equally good in mixed borders in large expanses of lawn, or under trees at the back of a lawn vista. They can be grown singly in a bed or used in groups for bold color. Because they are so easy to grow and maintain, I feel that hydrangeas, especially *H. macrophylla*, could be used more in school grounds, at camping sites, industrial parks and cemeteries. Locations such as these require a tough, long-flowering shrub, especially a summer-flowering shrub.

In all of these situations there is usually insufficient time or money to spend on colorful displays of annual bedding plants or herbaceous borders. The hardy, easily pleased hydrangeas will

Left: A hydrangea stands the test of time as a memorial.

Hydrangea opuloides with the pink *H. macrophylla* 'Princess Beatrix' (left) in a woodland setting.

give summer-long color at minimal expense. Should the shrubs be damaged or vandalized, they will quickly recover. That they get so few pests and diseases also helps in these situations, as the plants can be left to their own devices without the need for spraying.

On school grounds, for instance, the caretaker does not have the time to cultivate large flowerbeds, and the risk of damage from children's ball games would make this a thankless task. Likewise, shrubs such as roses have thorns and need constant spraying with chemicals, which we would rather keep away from our children, so the resilient are ideal for such sites.

CHAPTER 7

Climatic Requirements

You've decided you want to grow hydrangeas. Now you have to consider whether your garden is suitable for these shrubs and, if so, which ones. Hydrangeas are very easy to grow and so it is likely you will be able to cultivate at least some of them. Choose the right sites in your garden for your hydrangeas and they will perform well and give you more pleasure.

Local climate and aspect

No one knows your local or garden climate as well as you. You can best decide which varieties to grow where. If you are new to the area and are still trying to discover what grows well, there are quick ways of finding out about local conditions without the expensive trial and error method of buying plants that may die. One way is to walk around your local area and see which plants are doing best. If a plant grows well for your neighbor, then it should grow well for you.

You can contact your local meteorology office for details like annual sunshine hours, annual rainfall and its spread, i.e. does it occur evenly throughout the year or are there drought or dry periods. Records of temperatures, and especially the number and frequency of frosts, are important. Remember late frosts are always more damaging to plants than frosts in midwinter when plants are truly dormant.

The weather office can also give you a clue as to how windy your area is. Wind can be a major factor in deciding which plants will thrive in your garden.

Opposite: *Hydrangea macrophylla* 'Enziandom' (syn 'Gentian Dome')

Some plants have a very low tolerance to wind, while others are much tougher. Within the hydrangea group, plants range from the very tough, wind hardy *H. macrophylla*, some of which will stand up to a coastal gale, through to the more delicate *H. quercifolia* and *H. paniculata* types.

If there is a local gardening club or similar organization, this will be a good place to find some knowledgeable people with local expertise who can help you decide which plants will grow well for you. Most gardeners are only too willing to share their knowledge. Local nurseries and garden centers are other sources of knowledgeable plant people willing to guide you with plant choice and details of your local climate.

Let us look at the various aspects of climate and how they will affect hydrangeas.

Sun and shade

Hydrangeas are by nature woodland plants and are happiest in such settings. In nature they grow in either full sun or the dappled shade of deciduous trees. They will not thrive if the sun is shaded out by dense evergreen trees. In general, the more sun that they receive, the better they will flower. Adequate sunlight also reduces the number of pests and diseases likely to be a problem. Pests such as thrips tend to thrive in shade and so do some of the diseases like mildew.

In a moist climate the species hydrangea, such as *H. aspera quercifolia* and *H. paniculata*, do well in full sun. In hotter, dry climates it may be wise to give them a small amount of shade to keep the plants from drying out too quickly and also prevent the flowers from wilting or scorching. The hybrid macrophylla and serrata types are happy in sun or shade in a moist climate. Do remember that the mophead varieties need more moisture to sustain their flowers than the less bulky lacecaps. Again, a hot climate may mean placing these hybrid types in shade to prevent wilting and sun-scorch. In full sun any plant dries out much more quickly. One answer to this is to apply mulch, which will conserve moisture for the plant to use. Another possibility is the use of irrigation – perhaps you can install a permanent drip line around a part of your garden to keep the choice plants in good condition. Sun or shade is a factor when considering frost. Shady sites are usually less frosty.

Frost and cold

Regions with a continental climate have extremely hot summers, which have the advantage of ripening the stems of shrubs, enabling hydrangeas to cope with the upcoming winter. Piping hot continental summers are often followed by very cold winters, with a definite period of cold before spring begins. Once spring has sprung, the possibility of frost recedes. This predictable climate suits many plants as they "know where they stand", so even if the winter is horrendously cold, when it is over it really is over.

Other climates have winters that drift on and on. The weather can be warm one day and freezing the next and there is always the likelihood of a late frost. Plants such as hydrangea will come into growth as soon as there is any spell of warm weather, but if growth commences and then there is a late spring frost, the buds or leaves can be killed.

It takes a pretty severe frost or period of cold to kill a hydrangea, but shrubs can be badly damaged and perhaps not flower the following summer. If you have lived where you are for two or more winters, you will know the exposed or coldest parts of your garden. Generally frost flows downhill unless impeded by something like a hedge. The lowest point on a slope is usually the coldest. You can use this to good advantage by planting all the things that prefer a cold climate in the colder parts of the garden. Peonies, for instance, love a cold spot, so you plant them in the cold hollows where the frost collects. If you have a flat garden then you may think you do not have these options. However, some spots in your garden will be warmer than others. A "hot spot" may be a sun-trap by a fence or sunny wall. Buildings, especially those made of brick and stone, absorb heat in the daytime and give off radiant heat at night. This heat may just be enough to keep the frosts away from choice plants.

Hydrangea species like *H. arborescens*, *H. aspera*, *H. heteromalla* and *H. paniculata* are happy in winter cold. The hybrid macrophylla and serrata types are less tolerant of frosts, especially late frosts that can kill the emerging flowerbuds. Most *H. macrophylla* shrubs only bear flowers on the terminal or top growth buds and if these are killed by frost then the plant may not flower that summer, or its flowering will be delayed until the new growth with more flowerbuds can be produced.

One practical way to overcome this problem in an area susceptible to late frost is to delay pruning the bush until all risk of frost is past. When the plant is left intact, its general bushiness gives it some frost protection. Another option is not to prune the bush at all, giving the plant natural protection from frost, but you should tidy off the dead flowerheads in spring. These heads will last all the next summer if you leave them and ruin the attractiveness of the plant. If a bush is pruned it produces fewer flowers but each flower will be bigger. Left unpruned, the bush is furnished with lots more flowers but they are smaller because of the competition for water and nutrients.

The recently developed Swiss hybrid lacecaps known as Teller hybrids are considered by many people to be frost tender and not tolerant of cold winters, but I am told by Swiss nurserymen that these hybrids, like many other *H. macrophylla* cultivars, will tolerate winter temperatures down to 14°F (-10°C).

Hydrangea paniculata

I think the problem arises in areas where a spring frost can be immediately followed by an extreme drop in temperature, unlike Switzerland where cold temperatures are experienced in the depths of winter and not in spring. Maritime climates, for example, have indeterminate weather that swings from winter to spring and back to winter again the next day. The warm days encourage the sap to flow and the plant begins to grow, only to be hit by cold weather again a week later. It is this fluctuation which kills or damages the plants, and is why gardeners with maritime climates have such problems growing plants from cold regions of the world such as northern China and Korea. There, winters are much colder, but winter is winter and spring is spring and the two do not usually overlap.

In general, *H. paniculata* will grow to Zone 3, *H. quercifolia* will grow to Zone 5. *H. macrophylla* and *H. serrata* will mostly grow to Zone 5 or 6, though some are more frost tender and need Zone 8. In each case, the different forms of hydrangea will cope with sheltered inland sites as long as it is not too cold, although the big soft-leafed *H. macrophylla* may need careful siting in places.

In the U.S.A. and southern Canada, hydrangeas will grow in many regions. Areas with late frosts will be the most difficult sites. Either choose a sloping site so the frost flows away or find some overhead shade to protect the shrubs. Late pruning is the other technique for reducing frost damage in such areas.

Temperate coastal regions are ideal for hydrangeas though in more northerly coastal regions wind is more of a problem. Inland, hot dry areas or those

Hydrangea macrophylla 'Pia'

of extreme heat or cold make growing hydrangeas a bit more difficult.

Wind

Windy sites are often a problem for gardeners and this is especially true near the sea. However, a coastal situation is the natural home of many hydrangea species, therefore they are suited to a moist and windy climate. Many of the *H. macrophylla* types are extremely wind-tolerant and can be seen growing on clifftops; they are tolerant of salt as well as wind. Again, these same plants would excel if given a protected site. While I would not recommend them for the "teeth of a gale", hydrangeas will certainly tolerate more wind than most other shrubs. If you pick the right variety, it will cope with coastal gales. *H.m.* 'Seafoam' is appropriately named and is especially tough in a wild and windy site. *H.m.* 'Otaksa' and *H.m.* 'Ayesha' are also supremely frost hardy in these conditions.

If you can somehow mulch the plants or irrigate them in such sites, they will cope much better with the harsh conditions. Strong winds cause damage to plants in two ways. One is by physical damage to leaves and the breaking of branches. The other is more a gradual process whereby wind robs the plants of moisture. A plant naturally takes up moisture from its roots into the stems and then the leaves. Some of this moisture is lost through transpiration, where water in the form of vapor is lost through the pores of the leaf. ("Pores" are the "breathing holes" found on the underside of the leaf.)

As there are cushions of air around the pores beneath the surface of the leaves, moisture is normally lost slowly. In windy conditions this moisture loss is increased as there is no cushion of air around the leaves. Sometimes the moisture loss can be greater than the amount a plant can absorb through its roots. This may be because the plant cannot keep up with the moisture loss through the leaves or it may be that the soil is getting dry and lacks enough moisture for the plant to draw on. Eventually, if the plant cannot access enough moisture to keep up with the loss caused by wind evaporation, the leaf will wilt, and if the situation lasts for too long or is too frequent, the leaf may eventually crumple or burn.

Plants that can cope with wind have certain mechanisms to reduce water loss. These include hairy or glossy leaves, or a reduction in leaf size so that there is less area to lose moisture from. Hairy leaves, such as that of *H.a. villosa*, have formed their own protection, for the much-needed cushion of air around the leaf pores exists within the sheltered hairy parts and so water loss is reduced. The bristly nature of the leaf also makes them much tougher.

Shiny, stiff and glossy leaves found on *H. macrophylla* types likes 'Seafoam' mean that they are much less likely to be physically damaged by wind force. Shiny leaves lose less moisture because the wind cannot batter them or draw moisture from them as easily as from soft leaves.

There are several things you can do to help the plant overcome the problem of moisture loss. One is to provide a mulch of woodchips or bark, which helps keep the soil moist by reducing evaporation from its surface. Wind also removes water from the soil as well as from the plant. Another possibility is to install a permanent irrigation system so you can top up the soil moisture.

Rainfall

In general, hydrangeas come from high rainfall areas either in mountainous regions of China or North America, or from coastal regions of Japan and Korea. *H. macrophylla* is an especially thirsty plant, with big leaves and big flowers to keep supplied with moisture. Those varieties with lacecap flowers, being smaller in volume, require less moisture than the big bulky mopheads. Generally, such types are going to thrive in areas of high rainfall, but if you live in a low-rainfall area you can improve the chances of growing good hydrangeas by mulching and various watering methods. (See Chapter 8 for more about this.)

Hydrangeas will grow just about anywhere with a coastal climate, as long as it is not too dry. The biggest problem is likely to be with windy sites. The species like *H. aspera*, *H. heteromalla*, *H. quercifolia* and *H. paniculata* all prefer a sheltered site. *H.a.* var *villosa* is probably the toughest of these, having a rough, hairy leaf. *H. paniculata* 'Grandiflora' is especially sensitive to wind and needs a very sheltered site because the heavy flowerheads are easily broken. The more commonly grown *H. macrophylla* types are very wind-tolerant and are some of the best and toughest shrubs for exposed sites. Having said that, I must admit, *H. macrophylla* still performs better if given favorable growing conditions with ample moisture to supply its large leaves and flowers.

Hydrangea quercifolia, while it can survive cold winters, only flowers well where summers are warm.

CHAPTER 8

Soils, Feeding, Mulching and Watering

Soil

Like most plants, hydrangeas perform best in rich, loamy soil with plenty of available moisture. If your garden does not meet these criteria, do not worry, because despite preferring good soil, hydrangeas will also tolerate poorer ones. For most of the species the drainage does need to be good, but the popular macrophyllas will grow in wet and even waterlogged soils, though this may change the flower color. (I have *H.m.* 'Ayesha' colored soft- to mid-blue in my garden, but I also have a single plant of the same variety in a streambed and the flowers are distinctly pink even though the runoff water is acidic.) While I would not recommend you purchase a shrub to plant in a waterlogged soil, as you may lose it, macrophyllas are easy to propagate and you could take some cuttings and raise your own plants for those difficult sites.

The hydrangea species like *H. arborescens*, *H. aspera*, *H. paniculata* and *H. quercifolia* are not so forgiving about waterlogged or wet soils. They will, however, grow in poor, rocky or clay soils as long as they are reasonably well-drained.

Drainage

It is possible to improve poor soil and poor drainage. For instance, tough clay soil can be opened up in several ways. One method is to add gypsum (calcium sulphate), a safe kind of lime that makes soil particles lump together and improves the drainage. In clay soils all of the tiny little clay particles are spread like butter, preventing water from percolating through. Gypsum draws the particles together to

Opposite: Hydrangea macrophylla 'Mme Baardse'

form lumps like crumbly cheese and this allows more water and air to penetrate. Gypsum is regarded as "safe" because it is a form of lime which is acceptable to acid-loving plants such as rhododendrons, and it does not change the pH of the soil. Gypsum is the only form of lime with this ability to improve a soil's structure and drainage. Dolomite lime is another "safe" form of lime which has the added advantage of releasing magnesium, an essential plant element.

Another way to improve both the soil quality and the drainage is to add lots of organic matter. Old leaves, compost and farm manure are all wonderful for the garden, though take care when adding farm manure directly around plants as it may damage them through being too rich. It is probably best to rot the farm manure in a compost bin if you want to use it directly around plants. Chicken manure is especially strong and dangerous to plants in its raw form. Sheep, cattle and horse manures are all fairly safe. We once had a vegetable garden on such hard-packed clay you could dig up blocks to make adobe bricks. By adding horse manure from the local stables for two years and just laying it on the surface, we improved the soil to such an extent you could dig that vegetable garden with your hands. The worms and all the tiny soil fauna had done the work for us, turning the rich organic matter into humus.

By improving a soil's drainage we do two things: excess moisture is allowed to run away through the ground, which prevents the plant roots from becoming waterlogged; and it improves the aeration. We tend to ignore the fact that plant roots need air as much as they need moisture. (This is why, for example, it is so important to have a good open potting mix for our container plants. When the mix packs down, the poor plant suffocates from lack of air.)

Organic matter and compost are just as vital to a poor sandy soil which has little or no goodness. Here the drainage is fine but the plant is struggling to get any nutrients from the ground. The organic matter and compost will feed the soil and the plants.

If your soil is very badly drained then you may have to resort to digging trenches and laying drains to take away excess moisture. Laying drains is a very costly exercise and it tends to damage the soil structure; even digging can ruin this structure. It is better to work with nature, adding compost and organic matter, and then letting the soil fauna improve the structure and the worms improve the drainage.

Soil acidity or alkalinity

Hydrangeas are unique plants in that the flowers of the macrophylla types will change color depending on the acidity or alkalinity of the soil. Acidic soils produce blue flowers and alkaline or lime soils give pinks and reds. In theory, we can be artists with hydrangeas and create the palette of colors we wish. In reality, it is quite difficult to change the pH or acidity of soil in the garden, but we can easily manipulate soils in tubs and pots to give us a range of colors we desire.

Sometimes it takes several years for a hydrangea to become a fixed color in a garden. We planted a group of *H.m.* 'Gentian Dome', which is reputedly a good blue. It was pink the first year of flowering. Gradually over the years it changed from pink to mauve to an electric blue. You may buy what is described as the best blue, only to find it is pink in your soil. If your soil is acidic then gradually the plant will become established and give you the dazzling blue you wanted.

Why does this happen? Well, no one really knows why, but we do know how. Soil acidity is measured in pH units. A pH of 7 is neutral (neither acidic or alkaline). Above 7 is alkaline and the higher the

number, the more alkaline it is. Below 7 is acidic and the lower the number, the more acidic. The pH scale is a logarithmic scale, so pH 6 is ten times more acidic than pH 7, pH 5 is therefore ten times more acidic than pH 6. So pH 5 is therefore 100 times more acidic than pH 7. Most soils are between 4.5, which is very acidic, and 7.5, which is very alkaline and only found in limestone-rich areas. Yes, there are intermediates between each large number and thus 6.4 is more acidic than 6.5. (Remember we go down the scale for acidity and for blue hydrangeas.) There are pH test kits available from garden centers, if you want to measure the pH of your soil.

Acidic soils = blue flowers for hydrangea, and alkaline or lime soils = pink or red flowers. In reality, pH 6.5 will give reasonable reds and pinks, even though this is slightly acidic.

Hydrangea macrophylla 'Red Star' is a magnificent blue in acidic soil, making a mockery of its name.

Before you rush out and try to change your soil to acquire the brilliant blues or red flowers you have always wanted, take a moment to ponder why you want to make these changes. In my experience, gardeners always want what they cannot have. I know gardeners with alkaline soil who grow superb red hydrangeas, but are they satisfied? No, they want blue ones. They would willingly pay twice as much for the plant if you could "make" it blue. Likewise, people in areas with acidic soils would give their eye-teeth for pinks and reds. The area where we live has very acidic soil and grows fantastic blue hydrangeas, but all the locals want pinks and reds. Years of gardening experience has taught me to work

with nature rather than try and fight it. It is much easier to grow *H.m.* 'Nightingale' or *H.m.* 'Blaumeise' for fabulous blues in acidic soil, or choose *H.m.* 'Fasan' and *H.m.* 'Zaunkönig' for splendid pink and reds if you have alkaline soil than to try to change the soil and end up with wishy-washy or unpredictable colors.

Many hydrangeas are wonderful whatever the soil. The whites are white, of course, wherever they are. The serrata types like 'Grayswood' and 'Preziosa' change from white to pink to red regardless, and some macrophylla types like 'Merrit's Supreme' and 'Président Doumer' display wonderfully rich colors in any soil, though they will vary.

Feeding

A spring feed with a balanced fertilizer containing high nitrogen is a good idea. *H. macrophylla* types are quite greedy plants and appreciate an annual application in spring. If possible, spread the fertilizer before rain, so it will wash into the ground. Apply any compost or well-rotted farm manure available

Fig. 1: pH range in soils

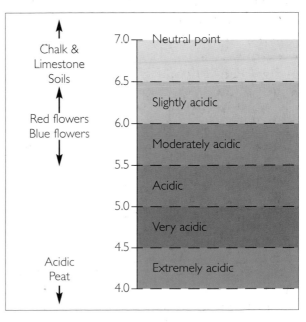

in spring. No need to dig it in – let the worms and soil fauna break down the organic matter for you. Avoid feeding the plants in late summer as it only encourages soft growth that is at risk of being frosted. Plants do not need feeding in winter.

Feeding to get blue flowers

If you have acidic soil you will be able to grow magnificent blue hydrangeas. (If you or your neighbors can grow rhododendrons and camellias successfully, you can be confident you have acidic soil.) As mentioned already, hydrangeas may take up to three years to settle into a permanent color. You can speed up this process by feeding them aluminum sulphate. If you are determined to change the pH of your soil to improve your chances of blue flowers the process is as follows.

To make your soil more acidic, you can add sulphur at 4 to 5 oz/yd^2 (125 to 150 g/m^2). This should lower the pH by 0.5, say from 7.0 to 6.5. Ideally this sulphur should be dug into the soil, but this may not be possible if the area is already planted. It will be easier and cheaper to concentrate on just one area of the garden.

Adding 8 oz/yd^2 (250 g/m^2) of aluminum sulphate will speed up the bluing process. It is free aluminum in the soil absorbed by the plant that turns the flowers blue. Beware that too much aluminum in one dollop can be dangerous to plant roots. "Little and often" is a good motto with this and other fertilizers.

Instead of sprinkling a year's worth of fertilizer on a plant in one go, with the risk of burning the roots or scorching the leaves, it is better to put on one-third of the annual amount three times a year. I know this adds to your workload but it is much kinder to the plant. I try to remember to feed my plants two or three times a year, between early spring and mid-to late summer. Feeding times depend on your climate. There is no point in feeding plants in mid-summer if everything is in drought mode. Plants need water to absorb fertilizer and if the ground is dry, this increases the concentration of fertilizer and thus the risk of damaging your plants. Fertilizer always works best with adequate rainfall or irrigation.

A fairly safe bluing agent for hydrangeas is potassium aluminum sulphate, sometimes called potash alum or just alum. It can sometimes be difficult to obtain and you may have to get it from a pharmacist. It has the advantage of releasing the chemicals slowly and so is safer for the plant.

A general fertilizer for blue hydrangeas needs to be high in nitrogen and potash, and low in phosphates. Avoid superphosphate as this makes soil alkaline. A good NPK (nitrogen (N), phosphorus (P), potassium (K)) mix would be 25/5/30 or 5/1/6. This blend has 25 percent nitrogen. Ideally the nitrogen should be in nitrate form rather than ammonium. Nitrates are released slowly to the plant whereas ammonium forms of nitrogen are quick-acting and increase the risk of burning the roots.

The NPK are what we call the macro nutrients – the ones the plants need most of, a bit like our staple foods. For good health plants also need micro or trace elements. These are elements such as copper and zinc, which they need in minute quantities. Most soils naturally contain all these elements, including the NPK, but a top-up to improve the health of the plant is always beneficial. Natural fertilizers such as manure and compost contain these nutrients too.

The availability of various elements is controlled to some degree by the pH of the soil. Certain elements become unavailable to the plant in high pH or alkaline soils. What happens is the calcium in lime locks up certain plant nutrients, so while the soil has all the essential nutrients, they may not be released to the plant. A sprinkle of chelated iron is always a help, or you can add iron sulphate at 1 oz/yd^2 (20 g/m^2). Iron counteracts the effects of lime and allows certain elements to be more readily available to plants.

Hydrangea macrophylla 'Mrs Kukimo'

Feeding to get pink and red flowers

As noted above, in alkaline or limy soils aluminum and other trace elements are unavailable to the plant. It is aluminum and not iron, as formerly believed, that causes the crimson pigment in hydrangea sepals to turn blue. Iron plays a role in this by allowing aluminum to be available to the plant. Calcium and iron are antagonistic to each other (the presence of one negates the other).

If you have a limy soil, I would recommend you grow hydrangeas in the good reds and pinks and not persist trying to grow blues and purples as it is endless labor for poor returns. Pinks and reds can still be obtained in a slightly acidic soil of pH 6.5, and will be even better at pH 7.0. If you have a slightly acidic soil and want good pink and red hydrangeas, add lime twice a year to increase the pH. Remember "little and often" is always safer for the plants. Too much lime at one time can cause chlorosis which is when the leaves go yellow (and shows up the prominent green veins). Dolomite lime is by far the best form to use because it does not change the pH and so it is safe to use around acid-loving plants like rhododendrons and camellias.

An ideal balance of fertilizer for hydrangeas in alkaline soils would be NPK 25/10/10 or 5/2/2. A fairly high percentage of phosphorus helps the flowers turn pink. Phosphorus combines with aluminum, and the two elements combine in an insoluble form. This means the aluminum cannot be taken up by the plant roots and so the flowers will be pink. (Plants can only absorb minerals in soluble or water-borne form.)

Hydrangea paniculata 'Tardiva'

Neutral soils

Neutral soils will give you the luxury of being able to grow both pinks and blues. If you have a neutral soil then this is the procedure to grow good blue hydrangeas. Use a mulch of bark to keep the roots as moist as possible. Add humus or compost which will feed the plant and have an acidifying effect. Feed the plant with iron sulphate to allow micronutrients such as aluminum to be available to the plant. Aluminum sulphate is the vital ingredient to give blue hydrangeas but it needs iron in the soil to be available, otherwise the lime or calcium in the soil will lock it up.

Advice for the determined

Imagine you have acidic soil and you're keen to grow good pinks and reds. There are several possibilities. The easiest of course is to grow the plant in a tub or raised bed where the soil or potting mix can be doctored to give red and pink flowers.

The second option depends on your house construction. If your house has a concrete foundation, then the cement contains lime which is gradually leached into the soil. Plant your red and pink hydrangeas beside the concrete foundation and they will immediately have more free "calcium" available. You can add to this by feeding the plant with lime. (Remember the safest form of lime to use is dolomite, which has the added advantage of containing magnesium, essential for the greening of leaves.)

The third option is to lace a portion of your garden soil with lots of lime until the flowers gradually turn pink. This is unlikely to work if your soil is very acidic. An easier variation on this is to dig a large hole and line the sides with polyethylene. The hole should be at least 3 ft wide by 3 ft deep (1 m x 1 m). (Do not put polyethylene in the bottom of the hole or the drainage will be impeded.) Fill the hole with alkaline soil or potting mix. Because hydrangeas are fairly shallow-rooted, all the roots will be feeding in your alkaline mix and so the flowers will be pink or red.

If you live in a limy area and you're determined to have a blue hydrangea or three, then there are two possible avenues. Grow them in tubs or planter beds where you can import soil or potting mix of the correct acidity and so ensure the roots are not in contact with the local soil, or try the polyethylene-lined hole technique outlined above. Fill the hole with acidic soil or potting mix and plant your bush. You will still need to feed the plants with iron sulphate and aluminum sulphate every spring to keep good blues. Alum or aluminum sulphate can check the growth of young plants and should be applied sparingly to your new purchases.

The other thing to be aware of is the water these plants receive. Tap water in a region of alkaline soils is likely to be hard, lime-rich water. Collect rainwater in a barrel under your downspouts to use on your hydrangeas. Alkaline water is called "hard" and acidic water is "soft". An easy way to tell what type of water you have is to look inside your electric kettle. If the kettle has a thick white deposit over the element and on the walls you have hard water. This deposit is lime crystals.

Mulching

We have already talked about the wonders of mulches and how they save work and energy. Mulches suppress weed growth, retain moisture and reduce the need to water. Hydrangeas are like rhododendrons in that most of their roots are in the top layer of soil with just a few stronger roots going deeper to anchor the plant. If the topsoil dries out, the plant suffers from drought stress because most of the roots are near the surface. There may be moisture down below but the plant cannot reach it. One simple and cheap way to overcome this and save on expensive irrigation systems is to mulch the soil surface. Mulching keeps moisture in the soil by reducing evaporation. The sun evaporates moisture from a smooth soil much more quickly than it does from a lumpy surface and if we

Hydrangeas and rhododendrons in a woodland garden, showing the bark mulch (front left) to suppress the weeds.

cover the soil surface we reduce the evaporation even more.

Mulches reduce temperature fluctuation, keeping the soil temperature even throughout the year. Mulches also have the advantage of keeping weeds to a minimum. Most weed seeds need light to germinate and so by adding a layer of mulch you deny seeds the necessary light. The few weeds which emerge from a mulch tend to be bigger and better because of the reduced competition and the extra moisture below. To my mind this proves mulches work, as even the weeds that grow in such areas are prize specimens – and easier to pull out as a consequence!

Hydrangea macrophylla 'Parzifal'

Over the years a mulch improves the soil structure, making the drainage better and improving root growth. Instead of the soil surface being baked by the sun and pounded by the rain, it sits safely cushioned against the elements, moist, and often full of invisible organisms busily breaking down the organic matter to provide food for the plant roots. There may even be worms where no worms existed before.

Materials used for mulches include tree bark or timber peelings from sawmills. Make sure the wood peelings are not from timber treated with preservatives, which can kill plants. Some people use sawdust, but it has two major drawbacks: it can form a densely-packed layer which becomes dry and will not allow rain to percolate through to the plant roots, and it robs the soils of nitrogen as it rots quite quickly. Your plants will be starved of nitrogen and their leaves will go yellow, so you will need to feed extra nitrogen, most of which will be consumed by the rotting sawdust, which has first claim on any nitrogen.

Other mulch materials depend on what is available in your area. Suitable products are spent hops from breweries, also peach stones or corn cobs from canneries. Pea straw is good. Because peas are legumes, plants which make their own nitrogen, pea straw contains the latter. Barley and wheat straw are not so good as they rob nitrogen from the soil in the same way as sawdust.

One of the most pleasant mulches I've used is cocoa-bean husks from a chocolate factory. When laid out on the ground and watered to hold it in place, this mulch has a pleasing clean appearance and the most delicious smell of chocolate!

Many gardeners now make their own mulch with shredding machines which mash their prunings and garden rubbish. All mulches gradually rot down and this rotting process robs the soil of nitrogen. Add a slow-acting nitrogen fertilizer such as blood meal and bone to compensate for this loss. Because of this rotting process the mulch will need to be topped up from time to time.

Hydrangeas have lots of fibrous little roots near the soil surface and so one of the kindest things you can do for a hydrangea is to give it a mulch.

Watering

Hydrangeas are thirsty plants, especially the *H. macrophylla* types with their big leaves and large flowerheads. If your rainfall is annually low, then choose as moist a site as you can find. Watering the plants with a hose is a slow and rather unsatisfactory method, as much of the water is lost by evaporation. Sprinklers save time but have the same evaporation problem. Permanent trickle or drip irrigation is the most effective for the plant as the roots are thoroughly watered. Trickle irrigation also conserves moisture, as most of the water ends up in the ground rather than being lost by sun and wind action. Trickle irrigation systems are relatively inexpensive.

It pays to find out how acidic or alkaline your water supply is. Often municipal water is strongly alkaline and this will affect the flower color of your *H. macrophylla*, for example; it may be advisable to collect rainwater for potted plants if you wish them to stay in the colors they originally exhibited.

Fig. 2: Watering different soils using trickle irrigation.

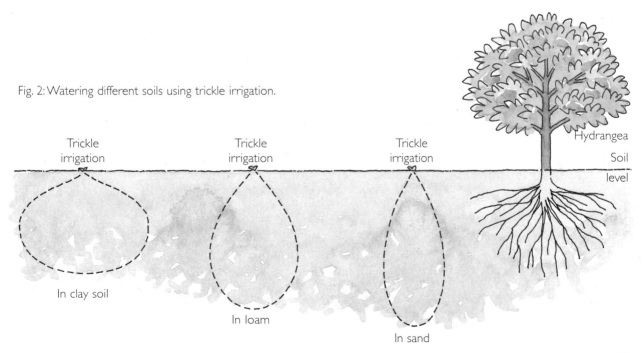

CHAPTER 9

Planting and Pruning

Plant selection

Whether selected from a garden center or mail-order catalog, your hydrangea should be of a type to suit your regional climate. It must also be a variety that is ideal for your garden for wind, sun, moisture and soil. Choose a hydrangea that gives you the color you want and a height that fits the proposed site. Most garden centers have a good range of hydrangeas, as they are popular plants worldwide. If you want something a bit out of the ordinary, it may be best to contact a specialist mail-order nursery.

Choosing the best plant

If it is summer and the plant is in leaf, then the foliage will indicate which is the best one. Rich, dark green leaves and general good health are the things to look for. If it is winter and there are no leaves, look for the best shape of plant, and good stout stems. For *H. macrophylla*, a vase or shuttlecock shape is best. *H. paniculata* may be grown as a vase or you may want to grow it as a half-standard, in which case you need a strong, straight central stem.

Hydrangeas are grown in both open ground and container nurseries. Open-ground plants are grown in a field and then dug up in winter and usually potted for sale. Container plants are grown in pots from the small cuttings stage to the time of sale, so all their roots remain intact within the pot. There is no preference for either, unless you are planting in late spring or summer, in which case a container-grown plant will transplant best as it still has all of its roots intact.

Opposite: *Hydrangea macrophylla* 'Nightingale'

Planting

Decide on the best spot for the plant, bearing in mind site specifics covered earlier in Chapter 7. Hydrangeas can be dug up and shifted later if you are the sort of person who likes to move their plant "furniture" around. However, the plant will be much happier if you choose the best spot for it first off.

Thoroughly wet the roots of the new plant before you start digging the hole by immersing it in a bucket of water until all the air bubbles cease. Dig the hole slightly wider and deeper than the pot, and pierce the sides and the base of the hole so the roots can easily penetrate the soil. If it is clay soil, it would be kind to dig a much bigger hole and incorporate some peat or well-rotted compost to give the plant a good start. Carefully remove the plant from the pot. Tease the roots which were at the bottom of the pot into a fan shape so they are ready to grow out into the soil. Some plants are sold wrapped in burlap, which should be removed before planting, but if the roots have grown through the material, it's wiser to plant the whole rootball. Just untie the burlap from around the stem and the rest of it will rot away in time. Place the plant in the hole and check to see that what was the pot surface is level with the surrounding soil. Getting this level right is most important for if the rootball is inserted too deeply, the lower part of the stem will be underground and subject to rot. If you plant it above ground level, the potting mix around the roots will dry out and the plant may die. After setting the level right, gradually fill the soil back into the hole and gently firm the loose earth around the plant with your heel.

The chances are that the plant will not need a support, but if it feels a bit loose or wobbly, then a

The bush at front has last year's dead flowerheads and needs trimming. The bush at the back has been trimmed.

stake or cane would be a good idea to keep it stable while the roots get established. Many shrubs are vulnerable to wind rock at this stage of their life. Water the plant thoroughly to help it on its way. Now is the time to add a mulch to control the weeds and conserve moisture. It is probably best not to feed just now; let the plant get established first.

From now on you will need to regularly check on the progress of the plant. Pull out any weeds that may appear through the mulch, and water if necessary.

Transplanting

You may decide to move some of your hydrangeas for aesthetic reasons, or because a plant is not thriving in its current site. Hydrangeas are very easy to transplant because they have a mass of fibrous roots near the surface. This means that when you dig up the plant you can take a large percentage of the roots and so it is unlikely to be killed or stressed by the move. Winter is the ideal time to carry out this operation, as the plant will be dormant.

Dig up and replant the hydrangea the same day; do not leave it lying out of the ground for any length of time. It does pay to prune the shrub quite severely so the reduced roots are not trying to sustain a large plant. It's probably easier to prune the plant before shifting it, as this will allow you easier access to dig up the rootball. Drastic pruning will also reduce the number of flowers for next year but this means less stress is placed on the plant. One peculiar habit of *H. macrophylla* plants is that after transplanting, their flowers will tend to be more pink or red, even if they were previously blue. This is because the plant has lost a lot of roots in the shift and finds it harder to absorb aluminum.

So, if you dig up and move a *H. macrophylla*, it will go pink, even if previously it was blue. It seems the blue coloration intensifies each year and by moving the plant you set it back into "pink mode".

Pruning hydrangeas

You may be surprised to find that not all hydrangeas require pruning, or need pruning in the same fashion. Each has its own special requirements to give the desired spectacular display.

Reasons for pruning

It is worth considering just why we prune shrubs. In general, we are inclined to regularly prune plants when in nature they are never pruned at all. We do this to:

1. Remove any dead and diseased wood for the health of the plant. (It always pays to do this before attempting any other pruning as this may alter the shape of the bush.)

2. Improve the shape, either to form the outline we desire, or maybe to open a bush to let in light and air. This increased light and air improves the health of the plant. Pruning for shape is a good idea in the early years of a plant's life, so it becomes an evenly balanced shrub.

3. Increase the number of flowers or the quality of those flowers. This is relevant in the case of hydrangeas, because, for example, if we prune *H. macrophylla* types we get fewer flowers the following summer, but each of these flowers is much larger.

Generally it is best to prune any shrub immediately after it has finished flowering, giving the plant a whole year to produce strong new growth for next year's flowers. Hydrangeas are one of the exceptions to this rule and are best pruned in winter, or at the very end of the winter or early spring if your area is prone to late frosts.

The pruning routine for popular varieties

Apart from an occasional tidy-up, *H. arborescens* does not need any pruning. The forms of *H. arborescens* such as 'Annabelle' and 'Grandiflora' can be pruned drastically to increase the size of the flowers. One method is to cut all branches to 1 ft (30 cm) from the ground in winter. Types which produce flowers from new growth make this technique feasible. The strong new growth produced in the spring will each have a large flowerhead on top of the stem. On a young plant these flowers need staking. A light pruning, removing perhaps a third to half of last summer's growth, will result in a tidier bush but slightly smaller flowers.

H. *aspera* var *villosa*, and *H. heteromalla* do not need any pruning apart from an occasional tidy-up every third or fourth year, and will not suffer in the least if they are never pruned, though you may wish to remove the dead flowerheads at some time. If you wish to prune them for shape, do so in the early years. A light pruning at this stage can be very useful, but beware of overvigorous pruning that delays the establishment of the bush.

It is a good idea to remove the spent flowerheads on *H. quercifolia* as they are so large and look untidy in winter. In general, *H. quercifolia* does not need any further attention, other than pruning for shape or size.

H. *paniculata* types can be left unpruned like those above, and this is probably the best course of action for *H.p.* 'Kyushu' and *H.p.* 'Praecox'. Hard prune the larger flowering *H.p.* 'Grandiflora' to obtain the spectacular giant blooms. Invigorate the

Fig. 3a: Pruning *H. paniculata* to a bush.

plant by cutting the previous summer's growth back really hard to one or two buds. In other words, leave just 1-2 in (3-4 cm) of last summer's growth. This drastic pruning forces the plant to create vigorous new stems, each one with a desired huge flowerhead.

A popular method of pruning *H.p.* 'Grandiflora' is to establish a short main trunk on the plant over the first few years of growth, then keep this the only permanent part of the plant. Every winter the long

Fig. 3b: Pruning *H. paniculata* to a half-standard.

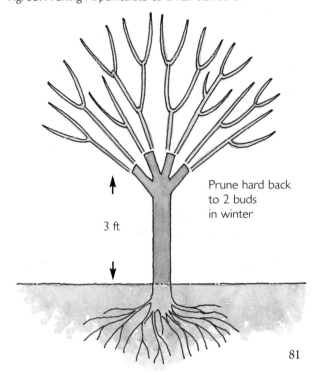

flower stems of the previous summer are cut back hard to one or two buds. From these buds strong new growth will appear in the spring and give rise to the gigantic blooms that make these 'Pee Gee' hydrangeas so outstanding. If you choose not to prune, then the plant will grow lots more flower stems and subsequently all the flowerheads will be smaller because of the increased competition for nutrients and water.

Pruning macrophylla types

The old flowers on a *H. macrophylla* go brown and parchment-like in winter. Some people regard this as a charming attribute and leave them as long as possible. Orderly gardeners just can't wait to chop them off as they see them as untidy. If your hydrangeas are blue, the papery flowerheads will contain a high level of aluminum, which is the chemical which turns them this color. It is a shame to waste this readily accessible aluminum by trimming off these dead flowerheads. Why not recycle this available aluminum by pushing the pruned heads back in under the bush? (You may need to weight them down with a log until they start to rot, otherwise they may blow around the garden like tumbleweeds.)

Dead flowerheads have a valuable role to play if you garden in a cold climate. The "froth" of spent flowers covering the bush acts as insulation all winter and protects the young buds from frost and cold. Wait until all danger of frost is past before pruning to the technique which suits your gardening style. You should however take off the dead flowerheads by late spring, to tidy the bush, otherwise they will last all the next summer and ruin the attractiveness of the plant.

In warmer climates it pays to trim off the old flowerheads on the lacecap varieties to prevent the plant putting all its energy into producing a crop of seeds. Lacecaps are less inclined to produce seeds in cooler areas.

Hydrangeas which are regularly pruned are the mophead and lacecap types of *H. macrophylla* and *H. serrata*. It should be emphasized, however, that they will not suffer if left unpruned. Young, recently planted varieties are probably best left unpruned, or just pruned lightly to make a good shape. Another possibility is to prune off any flowerheads so the plant puts its strength into making growth instead of flowers.

Timing is important when pruning an established bush, especially if you live in a cold region or your garden is subject to late frosts. Better to wait until late winter or early spring before pruning and then the bush is not tempted to come into growth too soon.

There are several ways of pruning *H. macrophylla*:

1. After long observation of the plant and its habits, this is the method of pruning hydrangea that I favor. Year one, a young plant produces a flower at the stem tip. Year two, it produces two flower shoots from side growths of this first stem. The number of shoots with flowers on from this original base stem will build up each year to 20 or so flowers. Eventually the wood gets old and exhausted. What I recommend on a large established bush is to cut out two or three entire old stems from as near to the base as you can. This has the effect of thinning the bush and reducing overcrowding. The plant will have fewer but bigger flowers next year, as there is less competition. Do this annual thinning every year in late winter or spring, depending on your climate and the likelihood of late frosts.

2. Many gardeners want to keep the bushes at a reasonable height and have a good display of flowers every summer. In this case you can prune lightly overall instead of just removing the dead flowerheads. Look for the large buds which are next summer's flowers. They are usually in opposite pairs near the tops of the stems. You need to retain as many of the fat flowerbuds as is practicable for the bush to flower well. Thin the stems, at the same time removing the weaker

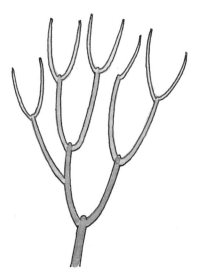

Fig. 4a: *H. macrophylla* branches produce more stems each year.

Above: Two fat flowerbuds in the center of the photo. The smaller buds below are growth buds.

Below: Pruning to the lower set of three pairs of flowerbuds. This will increase the size of the flowerheads. Leaving all six flowerbuds would result in smaller flowers.

growths, then reduce the height of the remaining stems, at the same time remembering to preserve enough flowerbuds.

3. Here, the idea is to prune the bush to increase the size of the flowerheads. This method will increase the individual size of the blooms at the expense of overall display, i.e. the bush will have fewer flowers but each will be larger. First remove all thin and spindly growth, generally cutting these out as low as you can go. You are now left with good robust stems. The next task is to prune these strong stems. Holding each stem in one hand and

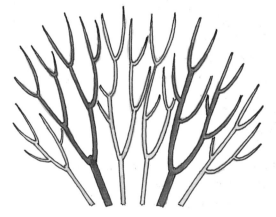

Fig. 4b: *H. macrophylla* bush thinned of some old branches at ground level.

Hydrangea macrophylla 'Blue Diamond'

secateurs in the other, go down the stem until you find the lowest set of big buds. What do these big buds look like? Near the top of the stem there will be fat buds the size of a fingernail, usually in pairs with one on either side of the stem. Occasionally there is only one fat bud with a tiny bud on the opposite side. The buds below these down to the center of the bush will be smaller buds which are growth buds. Each fat bud contains a new stem and a flowerhead in miniature. Supposing a stem has six fat buds, it will produce six small flowerheads during the summer and may be rather crowded. Pruning back to leave just one, or maybe one pair, of fat buds will give the large blooms we appreciate. Do this to all the stems and it is likely that you will be left with 15 to 25 fat flowerbuds for next summer's display.

The bush will also produce some flowerbuds from the tiny growth buds but these generally appear later in the summer, as the stem has to build up strength before it can flower. If you prune too drastically, you will delay the flowering in the following summer as the severe pruning will probably remove all the fat flowerbuds and the bush will have to make flowers from the growth buds.

Make your cuts flat, at 90 degrees to the stem, and prune just above the buds. Prune too high and the stem is inclined to die back, but this is not a major problem as it is with some shrubs, e.g. roses, which demand accurate pruning to prevent dieback and subsequent disease infections.

Climbing hydrangeas

These should not need any pruning other than to keep their shape. If you have a hydrangea growing up a house wall, then obviously you're going to have to prune it around the perimeters of the windows. Tidy gardeners may want to remove the spent flowerheads but as these usually disappear over winter there is no great need to get out the ladder!

CHAPTER 10

Pests and Diseases

Thankfully, hydrangeas do not suffer a great deal from pests or diseases. Compared to roses, which need constant attention and spraying to keep them looking good, the tough hydrangea can be left to its own devices for years on end without any serious ill effect. The species plants, such as *H. aspera* and forms like *H.a.* var *villosa* seem immune to pests and diseases. *H. paniculata* is equally trouble-free. *H. quercifolia* is sometimes prone to root rot, but otherwise has a good constitution. The few pests and diseases which do attack hydrangeas seem to concentrate on the *H. macrophylla* and *H. serrata* types. I stress the "few" as it is most unlikely you will ever need to spray your hydrangeas.

Pests
Slugs and snails
Slugs and snails are probably the most destructive pests of hydrangeas and they especially attack the *H. macrophylla* types. Slugs and snails love to eat the soft growing tips of young plants and can denude a small hydrangea. They seem particularly fond of the variegated forms of *H. macrophylla* and young, recently planted bushes. Control includes slug bait that can in turn harm birds and animals. Several environmentally friendly methods of control are cheaper and more satisfying. One is to sink a

Cover to keep out rain

Ground level

Beer

Fig. 2:. Slug trap

container, such as a tin can, with the rim at ground level, and part fill this with beer. Place a rough cover over the top to keep out the rain and also hedgehogs, which, like slugs and humans, are partial to beer. The slugs drown in a "happy" state and are easily disposed of.

Another method is to place moist organic materials, e.g. slices of raw potato or orange peel, around the plant. Slugs are attracted to these and can be found attached underneath during daylight hours and disposed of how you will. A possible deterrent to slugs and snails is a circle of gravel or grit around the plant as they don't like to travel over rough surfaces. A layer of pine needles would be similarly effective.

Spider mites
Spider mites are only a problem when hydrangeas are grown indoors or in greenhouses, or in very warm climates where the mites thrive in the excess heat. First you will see very fine webbing on the leaves, which may become distorted and take on a pale blotchy appearance. For a minor attack remove and burn badly affected leaves, then blast the plant with water from the hose. Spider mites thrive in hot dry conditions and hate frequent moisture, so an occasional blast with the hose or, inside the house, misting the plant with a spray of water once or twice a week, will both freshen up your hydrangea and deter the mites.

Mammals
As with many tender garden plants, deer, raccoons and squirrels occasionally eat the stems of *H. paniculata*, *H. arborescens* and *H. quercifolia*. As the plants

gain maturity, they seem to be left alone. A circle of chicken wire around the plant for two or three years is probably the best deterrent.

Thrips

These are an occasional pest in warm climates. They are tiny narrow creatures about the size of a pinhead. The juveniles are creamy yellow and the adults black. Thrips suck the sap from a leaf, reducing the general health and well-being of the plant. They leave a "muddy" deposit, which helps identify them. They prefer shade and attack plants in shade or the shaded parts of a bush. These pests are easily killed with a garden insecticide.

Cottony hydrangea scales

This is an uncommon pest and not one you're likely to encounter. When scales do attack a hydrangea, the bush can become heavily infested. You will see tiny cotton tufts attached to the stem. These are the egg sacs of the female insect. Scales suck the sap from the plant and have a hard case to protect them from predators and insecticides. You will need to add horticultural oil to an insecticide to kill them. The oil helps the insecticide penetrate the scale's protective case.

Diseases
Botrytis

This is a fungus that is more of a problem on young seedlings and cuttings than on mature plants. The appearance of gray mold or fluff is the first sign and it can be reduced, or hopefully eliminated, or better still, prevented, by good hygiene. Remove any dead leaves and spent flowers and prune off any dead and dying parts of the young plant. A disease that prefers a warm humid atmosphere, *botrytis* can sometimes affect young transplants. Reducing the humidity by opening windows will help to eliminate the problem for pot-grown or seedling plants. If *botrytis* becomes really bad, a fungicide such as a good proprietary rose spray will cure it.

Mildew

Most often a problem on plants grown indoors or in humid conditions, mildew is usually worse in shady sites. It can sometimes occur on plants in the garden, appearing in late summer and usually on plants that are under stress. With severe infestations there are little patches of dead cell regions in the leaf. Regular feeding, mulching and watering will reduce the likelihood of mildew attacks. If the problem is severe enough, an all-purpose rose spray will fix it.

Root rot

Root rot can sometimes affect the species hydrangeas such as *H. arborescens* and *H. quercifolia*. The most likely cause is *Phytophthora* disease, which is encouraged by wet soil and humid atmospheric conditions. Either try and improve the drainage or move the plant to a more free-draining area. Fungicides such as Ridomil (metalaxyl) may help prevent or cure the problem.

Honey fungus

This fungus can be devastating. It has honey-colored toadstools and often attacks the roots of trees that have been cut down to ground level. If you cut out a tree, the roots remain alive but stressed and this is when it is likely to invade and feed off the roots as a parasite. Plants that are not thriving are more likely to be attacked than vigorous healthy plants. Keeping your plants well-fed, mulched and watered will help prevent this problem.

Chlorosis

This is caused by a deficiency of certain minerals, usually iron. Plants growing in lime or alkaline soils are unable to take up enough iron and other micronutrients because the calcium in the soil locks them up and makes them unavailable. Apply aluminum sulphate and/or iron sulphate or powdered sulfur to remedy the problem. All these remedies will lower the pH of the soil and therefore make the iron

Mildew. The grayish leaf in the center is at an early stage of the disease. The brightly colored leaves have a more severe attack.

Chlorosis caused by lack of iron.

readily available to the plant. Beware of tap water, which can be highly alkaline in certain regions.

Wilting

This is usually caused by heat and lack of moisture, though it can be from root rot. Root rot is more likely to be a problem in wet soil, so if your plant wilts in the heat of summer, the probable cause will be heat stress. If possible, place a hose by the roots, turn the tap on very slightly and let a tiny trickle of water soak your plant over several hours. Long-term, add a mulch around the roots to conserve moisture, and perhaps install some permanent irrigation if this is likely to be an ongoing problem. Alternatively, you can move the plant next winter to a damper site.

Cold damage and frosts

These can kill the buds on *H. macrophylla* hybrids and this is especially true on young, recently planted shrubs. Remove any frosted buds that have a burnt appearance and are mushy to touch. Gently prune back to clean, healthy wood, just above a bud. Ongoing cold damp weather can have the same effect without there being a frost. The combination of frosted rotted buds and subsequent infections of *botrytis* can kill a young plant. Frequently a young plant suffers this problem in winter and is finally killed off by slugs eating the soft new growth in spring. Carefully select your planting sites and then keep an eye on what you are growing there. You hear gardeners described as having "green fingers" because of their ability to grow wonderful plants Usually they are just observant people who apply a speedy remedy to any problem. These same observers know their soil and the wet, dry or windy places in their garden, and choose plants accordingly.

Sun-scorch

This is a browning of flowers, which occurs when hydrangeas are grown in full sun without adequate rainfall or water. *H. macrophylla* needs lots of water to supply the big leaves and flowers. If the plant suffers from lack of water for too long the flowers dry and get sun-scorch, which turns the sepals brown. This effectively ruins the flower for the rest of the season and spoils an attractive head which could have been dried.

Viruses

Viruses are rarely found in hydrangeas. The symptoms are a narrowing and slight twisting of the leaves and also lengthwise streaks in the leaves. Once a plant has a virus it is impossible to cure. There are no sprays or other remedies because the virus is in the sap stream of the plant and impossible to eradicate. The only safe thing to do is dig up and burn the plant before the virus attacks any other hydrangeas. Viruses are spread by sap-sucking insects such as aphids.

CHAPTER 11

Propagation

Hydrangea macrophylla and *H. serrata* types are very easy to propagate from cuttings. Take these from the tip of a healthy stem during late spring to early summer. Remove the lower leaves and keep two to four leaves at the top of the stem. Cut just below a node at the lower end of the stem. If you have some plant-rooting hormone for soft to medium cuttings, then dip the base of the cutting in hormone powder or gel. However, *H. macrophylla* cuttings root so easily that this hormone is not essential. Pot your cuttings in a suitable mix and keep moist.

H. macrophylla will also grow from hardwood cuttings taken in winter. These can be placed in a pot or tucked in the side of a path or vegetable garden. Cuttings often root more easily if placed down the side of a pot or beside a concrete path

There are two reasons for this: the side of the pot or path will be slightly warmer than the surrounding soil; and there is more air available where soil meets pot or path and cuttings need air to root.

Other hydrangea species such as *H. aspera, H. paniculata* and *H. quercifolia* can also be propagated by the above method, though they are not as easy to grow as *H. macrophylla*. You can try soft to medium cuttings under a polyethylene bag, using rooting hormone powder or gel. Softwood cuttings either root quickly or die quickly – no half measures! Firm summer cuttings are more likely to succeed, as these have more strength and energy to call on for survival while roots are being produced.

Some species will grow from hardwood cuttings in the same fashion as for *H. macrophylla*. *H. paniculata* can be successfully grown in this way. When the bush is hard-pruned in winter you can use the hardwood bare stems. Trim each one just beneath a node and dip in hardwood rooting hormone. Cut off the top just above a pair of buds, making the cutting 8-12 in (20-30 cm) long. With a pencil or stick push a hole in the soil or potting mix and insert the cutting, taking care not to rub off the hormone from its base. Cuttings should be left for at least 12 months and either potted or transplanted afterwards.

The scarce *H. aspera* var *sargentiana* is tricky to propagate. One possibility is to layer it, or sometimes

Hydrangea macrophylla 'Harlequin' grown as a container plant.

Propagation. Stem at left showing rooted cutting. Next is a new cutting with just 2 to 3 leaves and cut below a node. Third one along is a cutting inserted in a pot, and finally a cutting covered with a polyethylene bag to prevent it wilting.

a plant will send up suckers from the ground, like raspberries. These can be dug up in winter and transplanted to form a new plant. Some of the other *H. aspera* and *H. heteromalla* forms can be layered to form new plants. Take a branch that is near the ground, preferably one which is slender and pliable.

Hydrangea macrophylla 'Heinrich Seidel' and birch trees.

Carefully bend this stem to touch the ground and peg it at this point so that part of it is kept in contact with the soil.

An even easier method is to place a brick on the stem, making sure there is enough of the stem tip, 8-12 in (20-30 cm), still exposed. The added moisture under the brick will encourage rooting. Leave the whole assemblage intact for a year, by which time you should have a new plant ready to separate from the parent plant. Only remove rooted layers in winter when the plant is dormant. Removing and transplanting the layer in summer will likely condemn it to an early death.

CHAPTER 12

Container Culture and Cut Flower Uses

Hydrangea macrophylla and *H. serrata* were originally bred to produce container plants for floral display and use for indoor decoration. Nurserymen began the practice of forcing them in greenhouses to make them flower earlier than normal and so increase their value and therefore their price.

The emphasis was on mopheads, as the lacecaps were deemed to have little value as container plants. Most of this breeding was done in France, Belgium and Germany. The plants are grown for a single season to produce one large or several smaller heads of flower which last a long time; the idea being that you have a colorful pot to decorate the house for several months and then throw it away when the flowers fade.

Hydrangeas are hungry and thirsty plants and this is especially so when their roots are confined to a pot. They need long-term slow-release fertilizers and frequent watering to keep them in tip-top condition. The easiest way to water is to place the pot in a plastic tray filled with water for the plant to absorb as necessary.

Sometimes hydrangeas are used to provide summer color in windowboxes and similar display containers. Pay keen attention to watering and feeding.

Generally it is much easier to produce good reds and pinks in pots than it is to get good blue flowers. If you want to produce blues, water a solution of $1/4$ oz/gal (1.5 g/l) of sulphate of iron and just a pinch of aluminum sulphate until the plant is established.

Pink and red flowers are easy to achieve in pots. A peat or crushed pine bark mix is likely to produce pink flowers. This may seem odd as both peat and bark are considered to be acidic mixes. However, they do not have free or "available" aluminum and so the flowers are pink. You can add a little dolomite or superphosphate to be sure of pink flowers.

Potted plants are often thrown away after a season but they can be planted in the garden, though they are unlikely to be the color they were in the pot as the acidity of your soil is unlikely to be the same as the potting mix. Hydrangeas can be used for longer lasting displays in tubs and large terracotta pots on a deck or other sheltered outdoor living areas. The containers need to be at least 20 in (50 cm) across.

Pay special attention to drainage. It is useful to cover drainage holes with large chunks of broken clay pots or stones. Fill with a suitable mix, leaving good space at the top for watering, and plant your selected variety in the usual way. In cold areas you can over-winter potted specimens in a greenhouse or even a shed as long as it is not too dark. Although the plants have no leaves in winter, their potting mix should not be allowed to dry out totally.

Hydrangeas as cut flowers

Hydrangea macrophylla and *H. serrata* types make wonderful cut flowers with their big, bold heads. A vase with three to five blooms of various hues is an impressive sight. *H. paniculata* and *H. quercifolia* types also make excellent cut flowers. If treated well, hydrangea flowers can last for two weeks in water. Small mopheads and lacecaps are generally more suited for cutting when blended with other flowers. Big mopheads dominate a vase and are best used alone.

Hydrangea macrophylla as cut flowers; 'Ami Pasquier' is red, 'Merritt's Supreme' is blue and 'Agnes Pavell' is white.

There is an art to keeping hydrangea flowers fresh and making them last. They have a tendency to wilt within hours of picking. Those with fairly short stems are best, as the longer the stems, the greater the wilting problem. Cut within the current season's green stems rather than into last year's older brown stems. Remove all the leaves except possibly the top pair. If you have lots of flowers to prepare, you can flick the leaves off by holding the head of the flower in one hand and running your closed hand down the stem from the neck. All the leaves will just "fly" off. Dunk the whole flowerhead and all the stem in cold water as soon as possible after picking. At this point it is probably best to trim off the bottom $^1/_2$ in (2 cm) of stem to have a fresh cut surface.

Dried hydrangea flowers.

Finding a vessel large enough to immerse the huge heads can be a problem. Possibilities include a large sink or a bath. You need to hold all of the stems and heads below water and, as they naturally want to float, use something as a weight on the stems only. Leave them immersed for at least an hour, preferably two. If you do not have a large enough container to dunk the flowerhead as well as the stem, then immerse as much of the stem as you can. Shake off the excess water before arranging them in a vase.

Sometimes the flowers may wilt again later. This may be caused by an air lock in the stem and can be remedied by cutting a small portion from the bottom of the stem, ideally with secateurs under water to prevent further air locks. If this fails, then submerge the whole head in water again.

Flowerheads cut early in summer are more likely to wilt. As summer draws on it becomes much easier to successfully cut hydrangeas; the nearer to fall, the better the heads stand up without wilting.

I'll leave the artistic bit to you, but hydrangeas can be used alone in a vase or featured as a bold centerpiece in a mixed arrangement. The heavy heads may need propping with wire, or rolled-up chicken wire can be inserted in the vase to give the arrangement stability and the desired shape.

Dried flowers

In the fall, after the heads have changed color, say from blue to burgundy or white to pink, is the time to cut hydrangeas for dried flowers. Some of the fall shades are fascinating: dark blues turn to wine-red and pale blues turn to green. The flowers change color in response to cool fall nights as the sap descends in preparation for winter.

Cut hydrangeas on a fine day when the flowers are as dry as possible, to prevent later rotting. Remove the leaves and put the stems in water. After a week or so the flower texture will change, becoming more rigid and paper-like. At this point you can throw away the water and the flowerheads will remain perfectly good throughout winter without any more moisture. It is possible to take longer stems for dried flowers than for fresh flowers as the water in the stems is not so crucial.

Some people recommend cutting the flowers and putting them in vases without water and drying them in a dry, dark, warm place for a week or two before using them in arrangements. Another method is to hang the blooms upside down in a dry shed for a week or two. Practice these techniques and see which works best for you. Hydrangea dried flowers will last for months. They will gradually fade a little, by which time it will be spring and you will have fresh flowers again.

Good varieties for dried flowers include 'Altona' and 'Hamburg' in the rich blues to wine and 'Générale Vicomtesse de Vibraye' and 'Maréchal Foch' in the paler blues.

'Otaksa' turns from a nondescript pale blue to a wonderful shade of pale green.

In the lacecaps, 'Lilacina' with its rich mix of colors, or the white-turned-pink 'Veitchii' and 'Grayswood' are all good subjects.

Appendix:
Recommendations for Special Sites and Purposes

Macrophylla hydrangeas for coastal gardens
'Altona', 'Ayesha', 'Beauté Vendômoise', 'Blue Wave', 'Hamburg', 'La France', 'La Marne' 'Lanarth White', 'Mme Emile Mouillère', 'Otaksa', 'Seafoam', 'Sir Joseph Banks'

Macrophylla hydrangeas for sun
'Agnes Pavell', 'Altona', 'Ayesha', 'Blue Wave', 'Lanarth White', 'Lilacina', 'Montgomery', 'Otaksa', 'Seafoam', 'Tokyo Delight'

Macrophylla hydrangeas for shade
'Immaculata', 'Maculata', 'Maréchal Foch', 'Mme Travouillon', 'Parzifal', 'Quadricolor', 'Socur Thérèse'

Outstanding blue mopheads (all macrophyllas)
'Blue Prince', 'Enziandom', 'Générale Vicomtesse de Vibraye', 'Hamburg', 'Maréchal Foch', 'Nikko Blue'

Outstanding blue lacecaps
H.m. 'Blaumeise', *H.s.* 'Blue Bird', *H.s.* 'Blue Deckle', *H.s.* 'Miranda', *H.m.* 'Nightingale'

Outstanding pink and red mopheads (all macrophyllas)
'Alpenglühen', 'Harry's Red', 'Masja', 'Merveille', 'Pompadour', 'Radiant', 'Satelite', 'Sontagskind', 'Westfalen'

Outstanding pink and red lacecaps
H.m. 'Fasan', *H.s.* 'Grayswood', *H.m.* 'Rotschwanz', *H.m.* 'Zaunkönig'

Passable reds in acidic soil (all macrophyllas)
'Ami Pasquier', 'Alpenglühen', 'General Patton' 'Harry's Red', 'Red Emperor'

Outstanding whites (all macrophyllas)
'Agnes Pavell', 'Bridal Bouquet', 'Immaculata', 'Libelle', 'Princess Juliana', 'Soeur Thérèse'

Outstanding hydrangeas, all soils
H.m. 'Ami Pasquier', *H.m.* 'Ayesha', *H.m.* 'Altona', *H.m.* 'Hamburg', *H.m.* 'Merritt's Supreme', *H.m.* 'Président Doumer', *H.s.* 'Grayswood', *H.s.* 'Preziosa'

Macrophylla hydrangeas for containers
'Adria', 'Altona', 'Blue Prince', 'Bodensee', 'Bridal Bouquet', 'Freudenstein', 'Harlequin', 'Immaculata', 'Maréchal Foch', 'Masja', 'Merritt's Supreme', 'Miss Belgium', 'Pia', 'Pompadour', 'Radiant', 'Westfalen'

Macrophylla hydrangeas for cut flowers
'Altona', 'Bouquet Rosé', 'Enziandom', 'Générale Vicomtesse de Vibraye', 'Hamburg', 'Maréchal Foch', 'Merritt's Supreme', 'Pompadour', 'Quadricolor'

Macrophylla hydrangeas for dried flowers
'Agnes Pavell', 'Altona', 'Ayesha', 'Europa', 'Hamburg', 'Lilacina', 'Merritt's Supreme', 'Otaksa', 'Princess Juliana'

Hydrangeas with scented flowers
H.m. 'Ayesha', *H.m.* 'Beauté Vendômoise', *H.m.* 'Seafoam', *H. paniculata* and *H. quercifolia*

Hydrangea species
H. arborescens 'Annabelle', *H. arborescens radiata*, *H. aspera villosa*, *H. paniculata* 'Grandiflora', *H. paniculata* 'Kyushu', *H. paniculata* 'Praecox', *H. paniculata* 'Tardiva', *H. quercifolia* 'Snow Flake', *H. quercifolia* 'Snow Queen'

Sources for hydrangeas

American Hydrangea Society
P.O. Box 11645
Atlanta, GA 30355

Boomkwekwerijen Nurseries
Fa. C. Esveld
Rijneveld 72, Netherlands 2771
XS Boskoop
Tel: +31 (172) 21-32-89
Fax +31 (172) 21-57-14
Website: www.esveld.nl
Extensive selection, many not offered in North America. Ships worldwide.

Bridgewood Gardens
PO Box 800
Crownsville, MD 21032
Tel: (410) 849-3916; Fax: (410) 849-3427
Website: www.bridgewoodgardens.com
Good selection. No shipping to AZ, CA, OR, WA or Canada.

Burncoose Nurseries
Gwennap, Redruth
Cornwall, United Kingdom TR16 6BJ
Tel: +44 120-986-1112
Fax +44 120-986-0011
Website: www.eclipse.co.uk/burncoose
Extensive selection, including some not offered in North America. Ships worldwide.

Country Gardens Nursery
36735 S.E. Powell Road
Fall City, WA 98024
Tel (425) 222-5616; Fax (425) 222-4827
Website: www.nwlink.com/~dafox/
Wide selection of cultivars. No shipping to Canada.

Corn Hill Nursery
RR 5, Petitvodiac, NB E0A 2H0
Tel: (506) 756-3635; Fax: (506) 756-1087
Hardy stock for colder areas.

The Crownsville Nursery
PO Box 797, Crownsville, MD 21032
Tel: (410) 849-3143; Fax: (410) 849-3427
Website: www.crownsvillenursery.com
Wide selection. Call for shipping restrictions.

Forestfarm
990 Tetherfine Road
Williams, OR 97544-9599
Tel: (541) 846-7269; Fax: (541) 846-6963
Website: www.forestfarm.com
Woody plant specialists offer many varieties. Ships to Canada.

Friends of the "Shamrock" Hydrangea Collection
Collection d'Hydrangea Shamrock
Route de l'Eglise
76119 Varengeville sur Mer, France

Gardenimport Inc.
Box 760, Thornhill ON L3T 4A5
Toll-Free Tel: 1-800-339-8314
Tel (905) 731-1950; Fax (905) 881-3499
Website: www.gardenimport.com
Varying selection from around the world. Ships to U.S.

Greer Gardens
1280 Goodpasture Island Road
Eugene, OR 97401-1794
Toll-Free Tel: 1-800-548-0111
Tel: (541) 686-8266; Fax: (541) 686-0910
Website: www.greergardens.com
Good selection, many H. macrophylla. Ships to Canada.

Heronswood Nursery, Ltd.
7530 NE 288th Street
Kingston, WA 98346
Tel: (360) 297-4172; Fax: (360) 297-8321
Website: www.heronswood.com
Extensive selection. No shipping to HI or FL.

Hydrangeas Plus
PO Box 389, Aurora, OR 97002
Tel: (503) 651-2887; Fax: (503) 651-2848
Website: www.hydrangeasplus.com
Exclusively hydrangeas, many rare varieties. Ships to Canada.

Wayside Gardens
1 Garden Lane
Hodges, SC 29695-0001
Toll-Free Tel: 1-800-845-1124
Toll-Free Fax: 1-800-457-9712
Website: www.waysidegardens.com
Excellent selection. No shipping to Canada.

Wilkerson Mill Gardens
9595 Wilkerson Mill Road
Palmetto, GA 30268
Tel: (770) 463-2400; Fax: (770) 463-9717
Website: www.hydrangea.com
Specialty nursery sells many hydrangeas.

Willowbend Nursery
4654 Davis Road
Perry, OH 44081
Tel: (440) 259-3121; Fax: (440) 259-3299
Website: www.willowbendnursery.com
Two- to seven-foot specimens, plus shrubs.

Woodside Gardens
1191 Egg & I Road
Chimacum, WA 98325
Tel/Fax: 1-800-473-1152
Website: www.woodsidegardens.com
Some rare cultivars. Contact about shipping to Canada.

Index

Bibliography

Coates A.M., *The Quest for Plants*, Studio Vista, 1969
Haworth-Booth M., *The Hydrangeas*, 5th edition, Constable, 1984
Haworth-Booth M., *Effective Flowering Shrubs*, Collins, 1965
Hillier H.G., *The Hillier Manual of Trees and Shrubs*, David & Charles, 1991
Krussmann G., *A Manual of Cultivated Broad Leaved Trees and Shrubs*, Timber Press, 1984

Lawson-Hall T. and Rothera B., *Hydrangeas: A Gardener's Guide*, Batsford, 1995
Mallet C., *Hydrangeas: Species and Cultivars*, vols 1 and 2, Centre d'Art Floral, 1994
Pizzetti and Cocker, *Flowers: A Guide for Your Garden*, Abrams, 1975
Tripp K.E. and Raulston J.C. *The Year in Trees*, Timber Press, 1995
Whittle T., *The Plant Hunters*, Heinemann, 1970